Complete Ho

Pisces 2025

Monthly astrological forecasts for 2025

TATIANA BORSCH

Translated from Russian by Sonja Swenson and Alexander Viner
Edited by Alexander Viner

AstraArt Books is an imprint of Coinflow limited, Cyprus
Published by Coinflow Limited, Cyprus
For queries please contact: tatianaborsch@yahoo.com

ISBN: 978-9925-609-82-6 (print)
ISBN: 978-9925-609-83-3 (ebook)

Contents

Astrological Insights into 2025: A Year of Challenges and Opportunities

The year 2025 will continue the challenging period that began in 2020 with the onset of the Age of Aquarius, as I mentioned in my 2020 forecast. The year can be roughly divided into two very different phases. The first half of 2025 will be marked by instability, struggles, and crises, both economically and politically. However, the second half of the year promises to be more positive and stable, with many problems gradually being resolved, the economy beginning to recover, and political issues starting to be addressed.

Starting in January, Jupiter, the most powerful planet in our solar system, will be in the sign of Gemini and will form several unfavorable aspects with Saturn during the first half of the year. Jupiter symbolizes new trends, while Saturn represents outdated state and economic systems. Their conflict signifies a battle between the old and the new. The old system has run its course and must give way to the new. However, obsolete political and economic structures rarely surrender without a fight, leading to fierce confrontations worldwide. This struggle is not confined to politics—new, often revolutionary trends will impact many areas of life. In 2025, we will witness changes in the political landscape of most countries, as well as in the lives of many individuals. Old politicians will be replaced by new ones, a process that will benefit the world as a whole.

The most challenging months of 2025 will be January, February, and March, when the conflict between Jupiter and Saturn will be compounded by retrograde Mars, moving backward from December 6, 2024, to February 24, 2025. This could lead to unrest in many regions, particularly in England, the USA, and EU countries. We can expect large-scale demonstrations, political strife, and conflicts rooted in religious differences. These trends may begin as early as November-December 2024 and continue into the first months of 2025. During this same period, military conflicts in global hotspots may reach a critical phase.

However, from mid-March to June, a period of realization and stabilization will emerge—politicians and society will start to recognize the need for change. The second half of the year will be more favorable: although changes won't happen overnight and not in every area, the situation will begin to stabilize and improve.

I would like to note that from 2021 to 2030, many planetary alignments will mirror those of the 1940s and 1950s, a time that profoundly changed the world.

Economy

In the first half of 2025, the economic situation is expected to deteriorate significantly. A large-scale financial crisis that may have already started in the second half of 2024 is likely to continue, affecting all countries worldwide. The second half of 2025, however, is expected to be much calmer, with the gradual recovery of the global economy from the crisis.

China will continue to be one of the world's economic leaders, with its influence on global processes growing noticeably. Domestically, the popularity of Chinese leader Xi Jinping will increase. However, the economic rivalry between the United States, Europe, and China will intensify, with China continuing to outmaneuver its competitors in the trade war.

India is set to undergo a year of restructuring. Measures will be taken to optimize the economy, and construction efforts will ramp up, yielding tangible results within two years, propelling the country into the future. Over the next three years, India will make significant strides in addressing issues such as poverty, and by 2030, it is expected to become one of the world's leading economies.

In the second half of 2025, businesses related to agriculture and food production will experience significant growth. Those involved in the dairy industry are particularly likely to achieve notable success.

United States

The United States will continue to face internal divisions. Pluto periodically returns to its position in the natal chart of the United States, a planet that is highly significant for the country as it governs the financial state and moral outlook of the population. Pluto symbolizes purification and renewal, but before it renews a system, it first destroys the old one. The 2024 elections will occur during a very tense time. In 2024, transiting Uranus will enter Gemini in the U.S. chart, and by 2027, it will occupy the same position it held during the Civil War. This suggests that societal polarization will deepen.

The 2024 presidential election in the United States will be extremely challenging. As I predicted in last year's forecast, Biden has exited the race: 'It is hard to imagine Joe Biden hanging onto the presidency. He will leave. I believe that Donald Trump will win, as Kamala Harris's horoscope appears weaker. This victory will lead to internal divisions within the country. (I am writing this prediction in July 2024, before my book is published, so the election results are still unknown.) However, I want to emphasize that the election period will be difficult for Trump as well, with many unpleasant surprises.

In 2025, the United States will continue to lose its standing on the international stage. The trend of weakening influence will become increasingly apparent and is likely to persist. This decline could result from failures on many fronts, where the resources to maintain the role of global hegemon are insufficient, and opponents will exploit this weakness.

United Kingdom

The United Kingdom will need to take decisive measures to stabilize its economy. Divergent opinions within the ruling circles may intensify the struggle between political parties, creating additional tension in society. A surge in public dissatisfaction, driven by the current political direction of the country, is also possible. However, thanks to Jupiter, the planet of luck, which will be in the financial sector of the UK's horoscope, significant progress in overcoming accumulated economic problems is expected in 2025.

The horoscope of the United Kingdom is based on several key dates. If we consider the founding date of the United Kingdom—January 1, 1801, when the union of Great Britain and Ireland took place—then in the next five years, we might see trends toward the disintegration of the United Kingdom.

European Union

The political and economic situation in Germany and France will be the most challenging within the European Union. Germany is still going through one of the most difficult periods, known as Sade Sati in Indian astrology. For Germany, this period primarily signifies economic decline and internal political strife. Conflicts based on national and religious grounds are also possible. This difficult period began in 2022 and will last for another 2-3 years.

Emmanuel Macron and his party will lose their position in France. However, even under Marine Le Pen's party in 2025 and 2026, neither prosperity nor even stabilization of the internal situation can be expected. External forces may actively hinder these developments. The economic situation in Italy also remains weak.

Russia

As I predicted in 2024, Putin remained in power after the presidential elections in Russia and began reshuffling the government.

In the first half of 2025, significant military conflicts are expected in Russia, which may involve countries beyond Ukraine, possibly including Europe and the United States. The Russian leadership will continue to change many people responsible for the country's economic and political development.

The West will continue to pressure Russia. The escalation of the conflict in Ukraine will continue in the first half of 2025, potentially reaching a more alarming level. Since this prediction is being written in the summer of 2024, it is possible to foresee that in the summer and fall of 2024, as well as in the winter of 2025, direct confrontation between Russia and NATO is not out of the question. The situation could become critical. However, a large-scale war could be prevented by factors unrelated to Ukraine, such as internal political struggles in Europe and the United States or major natural disasters affecting many regions worldwide, including the United States. It is possible that both scenarios could occur.

For Putin, the first half of 2025 will be extremely challenging due to unprecedented confrontation with the West. However, by spring 2025, it will become clear that defeating Russia on the battlefield is impossible. In the second half of 2025, Ukraine will be forced to cede Russian-speaking territories to Russia, and negotiations will proceed on terms set by Russia. These negotiations may continue into the first half of 2026.

Negotiations may also take place before this time, but without real results. The West will continue to demand territorial concessions and intensify sanctions and economic pressure, but this will not change the situation on the ground. Ultimately, some territories will be ceded to Russia, and this process may not always be peaceful.

Overall, the second half of 2025 will be more stable for Russia than the first. It will be a relatively good time for the country. Sanctions will, of course, remain, but events will slowly but surely begin to unfold in favor of the Russian Federation as the influence of the United States weakens under the pressure of its political and economic problems.

National policy in the Russian Federation will change, possibly necessitating the adoption of strict laws related to migration. This may occur due to terrorist attacks. December 2024, January, and February 2025 are particularly challenging in this regard.

Ukraine

It appears that by 2025, Zelensky may no longer be in Ukraine. What exactly will happen to him is difficult to say, but his situation will be extremely challenging. The period from December 2024 to February 2025 is particularly critical for him. It's hard to predict his fate, but he may be forced to flee the country due to numerous accusations, both from within Ukraine and from international sponsors.

In 2025, Poland may openly assert its claim over Lviv and other western territories, potentially deploying troops to these areas. My forecast suggests that Ukraine will be divided into spheres of influence, and I believe this division could begin as early as 2025. Hungary might claim Transcarpathia, possibly through a voluntary process like a referendum.

In the eastern territories that Russia has captured, the country will continue significant restoration efforts, rebuilding cities and infrastructure.

Middle East

As I predicted in my 2024 forecast, this year saw the outbreak of war in the Middle East. The situation in the Middle East, as well as in other "hot spots" around the world, is likely to escalate further. In the second half of 2024 and the first half of 2025, real conflicts may occur, not only along Israel's borders but also involving other countries. My prediction is that a ceasefire or peace agreement will be reached closer to the second half of 2025, but only after the situation reaches a critical point. In other words, things will get worse before they get better.

Technology

With Pluto entering the sign of Aquarius, which happened last year in 2023, various innovative technologies, neural networks, and artificial intelligence have gained significant momentum. It's worth noting that Aquarius is ruled by Uranus, which is associated with progress and unexpected changes, and artificial intelligence can be seen as one expression of this energy. We are also witnessing significant transformations in finance—mobile applications and electronic currencies are becoming increasingly widespread. Since Pluto will remain in Aquarius for about 20 years, the world will undergo profound changes during this period, and 2024–2025 will bring many unexpected technological breakthroughs. Naturally, this will impact space exploration, and we can expect significant advancements in this field in the coming years, potentially revealing much more about life beyond our planet.

Weather

The weather in 2025 will continue to deliver unpleasant surprises. In regions that have already suffered from floods, there is a likelihood of similar situations recurring, but on an even larger scale.

In the spring and summer of 2025, major wildfires are expected, so it's wise to prepare in advance. Saturn and Neptune will be in the fire sign of Aries throughout the summer, leading to an increase in the scale of fires compared to previous years.

In seismically active areas of the planet, earthquakes are possible.

Family

When it comes to people's lives, it can be said that the challenging planetary alignments in the first half of 2025 will affect everyone. How these aspects will manifest depends on individual horoscopes. For some, it could mean divorce; for others, professional troubles—each person will experience something unique.

The second half of 2025 looks more stable from an astrological perspective. The planets will calm down, and life will gradually return to normal. The second half of 2025 is a good time for marriage, childbirth, and acquiring property. People will begin to return to a proper understanding of family values, taking more care of their parents and elder family members.

Health

In terms of health, the first half of 2025 could also bring several unpleasant surprises.

Infections related to respiratory issues may reappear, as well as neurological disorders that could be difficult to diagnose. Those with chronic leg conditions may also face various flare-ups. Summer 2025 could bring exacerbations of cardiovascular diseases, migraines, and strokes. So take care of yourself if you have any predispositions to these conditions.

The second half of the year will bring new advancements—significant progress in technologies related to cancer treatment and various tumor diseases is expected.

During this period, people may become more concerned with various diets, leading to an increase in the production of organic foods, which will become more sought after.

Fashion

In the first half of 2025, fashion will be dominated by youthful trends and extravagant outfits. There may be some chaos, with a mix of styles that were once considered incompatible.

Since Jupiter is in the air sign of Gemini, lightweight, transparent fabrics, mesh, chiffon, and comfortable knitwear will be in demand. Colors will range from greenish-gray and bluish-gray to soft pastel shades.

In the second half of the year, as Jupiter moves into the sign of Cancer and forms a friendly aspect with Saturn, a return to classic styles is expected. Leather in various forms will become popular again, and denim will see a resurgence in various styles. Colors will include all shades of blue, black, and gray.

Travel

In the first half of 2025, I would not recommend long-distance travel or making important decisions regarding relocation.

In this regard, the second half of the year will be more successful.

For more detailed information, check out my forecast for the zodiac signs.

Good luck in 2025!
Astrologer Tatiana Borsch

2025 Overview for Pisces

Despite the pressure from Saturn, you are steadily moving forward. Don't stop, even if your path sometimes resembles a labyrinth. Your personal motto for this year is: "The road is made by walking!"

Business. In professional terms, this year can be described as difficult yet successful. Significant challenges are expected in the first few months, continuing the problems that arose in the fall and winter of 2024. Those engaged in expanding their business will face inspections, as well as stubbornness and incompetence from subordinates. Entrepreneurs and managers should closely monitor their surroundings, as there may be both covert and overt opposition. Employees need to be more attentive to their colleagues and superiors, as there will be those who want to take their positions. January and February are particularly challenging, but starting from March, the situation will stabilize somewhat.

It should also be noted that the first half of the year is chaotic, unstable, and full of surprises, mostly unpleasant. Influencing the situation will be difficult, so it's wise to review all weak points in your work and take necessary measures.

The second half of 2025 is calmer. During this period, it will become clear that you have successfully handled all the challenges posed by the stars and are steadily moving forward. The popularity of many representatives of your sign will noticeably increase—either within a narrow circle of specialists or with broader public recognition. The main benefits of the second half of 2025 will be stability and the restoration of previous connections.

During this period, relationships with colleagues from other cities or countries, which had significantly deteriorated in the fall and winter of 2024 and the first months of 2025, will be resolved. In the second half of 2025, everything will slowly but surely return to normal.

Money. Significant expenses are likely in the first half of 2025, related to work, business expansion, family problems, and household concerns. In the second half of the year, finances will improve, directly indicating success in business and stabilization in personal life.

Love and Family. For many Pisces, work will take a back seat, and significant developments can be expected in personal life. Various housing operations—construction, renovation, purchase of a new home—will occupy the entire first half of the year. Naturally, the atmosphere in many families will be tense and unstable, with financial and emotional difficulties disrupting peace at home.

In the second half of the year, the situation will improve significantly, and many families will welcome children or grandchildren. This period is favorable for lovers, with new romances and the potential for rekindling old connections. Those who quarreled in the past will realize that love still exists and forgive each other's grievances.

Health. In the first half of the year, the energy levels of most Pisces will be quite low. Therefore, maintain a healthy lifestyle and ensure you find time for rest. There may be a tendency to gain weight, so plan a diet, remember the benefits of exercise, and engage in moderate physical activity. In the second half of the year, energy will increase, along with your attractiveness, charm, and influence on others.

January

New York Time		
Calendar Day	Lunar Day	Lunar Day Start Time
31/12/24	2	7:54:20 AM
01/01/25	3	8:38:27 AM
02/01/25	4	9:16:49 AM
03/01/25	5	9:50:37 AM
04/01/25	6	10:21:18 AM
05/01/25	7	10:50:26 AM
06/01/25	8	11:19:31 AM
07/01/25	9	11:50:09 AM
08/01/25	10	12:24:01 PM
09/01/25	11	1:02:52 PM
10/01/25	12	1:48:21 PM
11/01/25	13	2:41:18 PM
12/01/25	14	3:41:05 PM
13/01/25	15	4:45:27 PM
14/01/25	16	5:51:26 PM
15/01/25	17	6:56:40 PM
16/01/25	18	7:59:54 PM
17/01/25	19	9:00:56 PM
18/01/25	20	10:00:16 PM
19/01/25	21	10:58:36 PM
20/01/25	22	11:56:47 PM
22/01/25	23	12:55:27 AM
23/01/25	24	1:54:55 AM
24/01/25	25	2:54:54 AM
25/01/25	26	3:54:21 AM
26/01/25	27	4:51:30 AM
27/01/25	28	5:44:26 AM
28/01/25	29	6:31:48 AM
29/01/25	30	7:13:21 AM
29/01/25	1	7:37:19 AM
30/01/25	2	7:49:50 AM
31/01/25	3	8:22:34 AM

London Time		
Calendar Day	Lunar Day	Lunar Day Start Time
31/12/24	2	8:32:59 AM
01/01/25	3	9:12:32 AM
02/01/25	4	9:44:09 AM
03/01/25	5	10:10:00 AM
04/01/25	6	10:32:08 AM
05/01/25	7	10:52:20 AM
06/01/25	8	11:12:10 AM
07/01/25	9	11:33:09 AM
08/01/25	10	11:57:02 AM
09/01/25	11	12:25:58 PM
10/01/25	12	1:02:33 PM
11/01/25	13	1:49:18 PM
12/01/25	14	2:47:15 PM
13/01/25	15	3:54:35 PM
14/01/25	16	5:07:10 PM
15/01/25	17	6:20:52 PM
16/01/25	18	7:33:09 PM
17/01/25	19	8:43:09 PM
18/01/25	20	9:51:07 PM
19/01/25	21	10:57:47 PM
21/01/25	22	12:04:04 AM
22/01/25	23	1:10:39 AM
23/01/25	24	2:17:49 AM
24/01/25	25	3:24:57 AM
25/01/25	26	4:30:17 AM
26/01/25	27	5:30:59 AM
27/01/25	28	6:24:05 AM
28/01/25	29	7:08:08 AM
29/01/25	30	7:43:37 AM
29/01/25	1	12 37:19 PM
30/01/25	2	8:12:21 AM
31/01/25	3	8:36:29 AM

You can find the description of each lunar day in the chapter "A Guide to The Moon Cycle and Lunar Days"

This month will be filled with thrilling moments, both in business and in your personal life. As the saying goes, "Everyone has their cross to bear."

Business. For those who are professionally active, January will be productive yet somewhat unsettling. The best time for you will be from the 10th to the 30th of the month, during which you might receive good news from afar or embark on a successful trip. You can rely on valuable assistance from friends or gain favor from influential individuals.

However, the first ten days of January might present challenges. During this period, managers may face significant issues with subordinates or unexpected disruptions in workflow. The situation may seem critical, so it's essential to review all possible options and take necessary actions when possible.

Workplace complications may also arise for employees, including hostility from colleagues and organizational difficulties. Many of you will need to address issues that originated in the past year, 2024. These might include disputes with partners over real estate and various financial matters. Resolving these issues will be a slow process, with improvements expected only in the second half of 2025. For now, tackle problems step by step, keeping in mind the wisdom of the saying, "A journey of a thousand miles begins with a single step."

Money. Financially, January can be described as turbulent. Expenses will alternate with income, but expenses may slightly outweigh earnings. Most spending will likely be related to personal life, family matters, and children.

Love and Family. Personal life might take center stage this month, bringing a number of challenges. Couples with longstanding difficulties may continue to address complex issues that originated in 2024 or even earlier. Real estate could become a major irritant and a source of disputes among struggling couples. In the most difficult cases, divorce, property division, and disagreements over child-rearing are possible. If litigation is anticipated, be prepared for the likelihood of a complex outcome and consider seeking a reasonable compromise.

For lovers and those who have just started family life, the situation looks more promising. However, they will still face various issues involving parents and older family members.

Health. In terms of health, both the first and last weeks of January look particularly challenging. The period from the 1st to the 6th may be prone to accidents and conflicts, while the days from the 28th to the 30th could bring a significant weakening of energy, as well as the likelihood of colds and infections.

Those suffering from cardiovascular, spinal, and musculoskeletal conditions should be especially mindful of unexpected complications during this time. Take care of yourself and prioritize your well-being.

February

New York Time			London Time		
Calendar Day	Lunar Day	Lunar Day Start Time	Calendar Day	Lunar Day	Lunar Day Start Time
01/02/25	4	8:53:02 AM	01/02/25	4	8:57:54 AM
02/02/25	5	9:22:45 AM	02/02/25	5	9:18:17 AM
03/02/25	6	9:53:17 AM	03/02/25	6	9:39:10 AM
04/02/25	7	10:26:12 AM	04/02/25	7	10:02:12 AM
05/02/25	8	11:03:11 AM	05/02/25	8	10:29:18 AM
06/02/25	9	11:45:49 AM	06/02/25	9	11:02:48 AM
07/02/25	10	12:35:12 PM	07/02/25	10	11:45:09 AM
08/02/25	11	1:31:20 PM	08/02/25	11	12:37:57 PM
09/02/25	12	2:32:46 PM	09/02/25	12	1:40:38 PM
10/02/25	13	3:37:06 PM	10/02/25	13	2:50:10 PM
11/02/25	14	4:41:55 PM	11/02/25	14	4:02:40 PM
12/02/25	15	5:45:37 PM	12/02/25	15	5:15:06 PM
13/02/25	16	6:47:32 PM	13/02/25	16	6:25:58 PM
14/02/25	17	7:47:46 PM	14/02/25	17	7:34:57 PM
15/02/25	18	8:46:47 PM	15/02/25	18	8:42:28 PM
16/02/25	19	9:45:14 PM	16/02/25	19	9:49:11 PM
17/02/25	20	10:43:42 PM	17/02/25	20	10:55:43 PM
18/02/25	21	11:42:34 PM	19/02/25	21	12:02:25 AM
20/02/25	22	12:41:45 AM	20/02/25	22	1:09:02 AM
21/02/25	23	1:40:37 AM	21/02/25	23	2:14:24 AM
22/02/25	24	2:37:53 AM	22/02/25	24	3:16:20 AM
23/02/25	25	3:31:54 AM	23/02/25	25	4:12:06 AM
24/02/25	26	4:21:14 AM	24/02/25	26	4:59:43 AM
25/02/25	27	5:05:13 AM	25/02/25	27	5:38:49 AM
26/02/25	28	5:44:08 AM	26/02/25	28	6:10:37 AM
27/02/25	29	6:18:58 AM	27/02/25	29	6:37:03 AM
27/02/25	1	7:46:43 PM	28/02/25	1	12:46:43 AM
28/02/25	2	6:51:05 AM	28/02/25	2	7:00:04 AM

You can find the description of each lunar day in the chapter "A Guide to The Moon Cycle and Lunar Days"

February presents a mix of success and challenges—essentially, just normal life.

Business. February is more suited for handling calm organizational tasks and personal affairs. Hardworking Pisces might tackle long-delayed projects. It's an ideal time to organize, plan for the future, or take a brief break to focus on personal matters.

Entrepreneurs and managers may continue expanding their businesses, possibly involving renovations or acquiring production spaces. Issues related to real estate are gradually being resolved, and you can expect some breakthroughs in this area.

Money. The financial situation is stable. With Venus, the planet of fortune, in your financial sector for most of February, you won't be short on funds. Expect earnings from both regular and unofficial sources. Some may receive financial support from family or secure a favorable loan. Profits from successful real estate transactions or banking savings are likely. Your expenses will be few and primarily personal.

Love and Family. Personal life will take center stage for many Pisces this month.

For those in relationships, it's a complex but interesting period. Old relationships may rekindle; partners who parted ways or fought might return apologetically. Whether reconciliation happens depends on your response. If you aren't too harsh, you can avoid further problems. The outcome hinges on past situations and the extent of transgressions on both sides.

Parents will devote time to their children, whose needs may require special attention and involvement. Another major theme is managing real estate matters—continuing renovations, buying new property, or selling the old, ensuring plenty of family responsibilities.

Health. Typically, the last month before your birthday is not great health-wise. You might experience a dip in energy, increasing the risk of infections, colds, and flare-ups of chronic conditions. Exercise particular caution with travel and driving from the 9th to the 12th. These days are also prone to conflicts and accidents.

March

New York Time			London Time		
Calendar Day	Lunar Day	Lunar Day Start Time	Calendar Day	Lunar Day	Lunar Day Start Time
01/03/25	3	7:21:59 AM	01/03/25	3	7:21:26 AM
02/03/25	4	7:53:09 AM	02/03/25	4	7:42:45 AM
03/03/25	5	8:26:13 AM	03/03/25	5	8:05:38 AM
04/03/25	6	9:02:46 AM	04/03/25	6	8:31:58 AM
05/03/25	7	9:44:24 AM	05/03/25	7	9:03:55 AM
06/03/25	8	10:32:14 AM	06/03/25	8	9:43:54 AM
07/03/25	9	11:26:30 AM	07/03/25	9	10:33:41 AM
08/03/25	10	12:26:05 PM	08/03/25	10	11:33:16 AM
09/03/25	11	2:28:53 PM	09/03/25	11	12:40:12 PM
10/03/25	12	3:32:40 PM	10/03/25	12	1:50:56 PM
11/03/25	13	4:35:49 PM	11/03/25	13	3:02:25 PM
12/03/25	14	5:37:34 PM	12/03/25	14	4:12:55 PM
13/03/25	15	6:37:51 PM	13/03/25	15	5:21:54 PM
14/03/25	16	7:37:02 PM	14/03/25	16	6:29:35 PM
15/03/25	17	8:35:37 PM	15/03/25	17	7:36:28 PM
16/03/25	18	9:34:07 PM	16/03/25	18	8:43:06 PM
17/03/25	19	10:32:51 PM	17/03/25	19	9:49:49 PM
18/03/25	20	11:31:47 PM	18/03/25	20	10:56:24 PM
20/03/25	21	12:30:21 AM	20/03/25	21	12:01:56 AM
21/03/25	22	1:27:31 AM	21/03/25	22	1:04:36 AM
22/03/25	23	2:21:51 AM	22/03/25	23	2:01:57 AM
23/03/25	24	3:11:57 AM	23/03/25	24	2:51:52 AM
24/03/25	25	3:57:03 AM	24/03/25	25	3:33:30 AM
25/03/25	26	4:37:13 AM	25/03/25	26	4:07:36 AM
26/03/25	27	5:13:10 AM	26/03/25	27	4:35:49 AM
27/03/25	28	5:46:09 AM	27/03/25	28	5:00:02 AM
28/03/25	29	6:17:32 AM	28/03/25	29	5:22:02 AM
29/03/25	30	6:48:51 AM	29/03/25	30	5:43:27 AM
29/03/25	1	7:00:07 AM	29/03/25	1	11:00:07 AM
30/03/25	2	7:21:39 AM	30/03/25	2	7:05:54 AM
31/03/25	3	7:57:39 AM	31/03/25	3	7:31:14 AM

You can find the description of each lunar day in the chapter "A Guide to The Moon Cycle and Lunar Days"

March may not be the best time to achieve outstanding results in either your professional or personal life. So, just go with the flow, and eventually, it will lead you somewhere.

Business. Entrepreneurs and managers at all levels will need to focus on financial matters — tracking expenses, recording income, and planning budgets.

Relationships with partners from other cities or countries are going well, particularly with long-established connections. Negotiations, trips, and plans to resume cooperation are possible.

For employees, things are steady, with everything moving along as usual, albeit perhaps a bit more slowly than normal. In fact, this slow pace may be noticeable for professionals across the board. Planned activities might be canceled or postponed, and key people may be unavailable for various reasons. This is because Mercury and Venus will be retrograde for most of the month, which usually leads to misunderstandings and delays in both business and communications.

Creative professionals, such as musicians, singers, and journalists, are likely to fare well, with plenty of work and decent pay on the horizon.

Money. Finances will take up much of your time and energy, but the effort will be worthwhile. Many Pisces will see an increase in income. The most likely dates for receiving significant sums are March 2, 3, 10, 11, 20, 21, 29, and 30.

Love and Family. For most Pisces, the key events in March will center around personal life. Parents will have more time to spend with their children, who will bring them some joy. Many Pisces will continue to focus on home improvements, and the stars advise approaching these tasks with great care, as the risk of mistakes is high this month.

Couples in love may strengthen their relationships and may even consider taking a trip together. March also holds the potential for rekindling old romances — an old flame might unexpectedly reappear, reigniting a past love with renewed passion.

Health. Your energy levels will be strong this month, and health concerns shouldn't trouble you.

One more thing — March is perfect for a break. Remember, the world won't collapse if you take a week or two off from work to indulge yourself!

April

New York Time			London Time		
Calendar Day	Lunar Day	Lunar Day Start Time	Calendar Day	Lunar Day	Lunar Day Start Time
01/04/25	4	8:38:31 AM	01/04/25	4	8:01:37 AM
02/04/25	5	9:25:37 AM	02/04/25	5	8:39:35 AM
03/04/25	6	10:19:23 AM	03/04/25	6	9:27:16 AM
04/04/25	7	11:18:50 AM	04/04/25	7	10:25:12 AM
05/04/25	8	12:21:47 PM	05/04/25	8	11:31:16 AM
06/04/25	9	1:25:48 PM	06/04/25	9	12:41:43 PM
07/04/25	10	2:29:06 PM	07/04/25	10	1:53:08 PM
08/04/25	11	3:30:51 PM	08/04/25	11	3:03:33 PM
09/04/25	12	4:31:00 PM	09/04/25	12	4:12:23 PM
10/04/25	13	5:29:58 PM	10/04/25	13	5:19:50 PM
11/04/25	14	6:28:20 PM	11/04/25	14	6:26:28 PM
12/04/25	15	7:26:40 PM	12/04/25	15	7:32:54 PM
13/04/25	16	8:25:19 PM	13/04/25	16	8:39:34 PM
14/04/25	17	9:24:17 PM	14/04/25	17	9:46:21 PM
15/04/25	18	10:23:07 PM	15/04/25	18	10:52:28 PM
16/04/25	19	11:20:45 PM	16/04/25	19	11:56:14 PM
18/04/25	20	12:15:44 AM	18/04/25	20	12:55:14 AM
19/04/25	21	1:06:38 AM	19/04/25	21	1:47:11 AM
20/04/25	22	1:52:32 AM	20/04/25	22	2:30:52 AM
21/04/25	23	2:33:20 AM	21/04/25	23	3:06:41 AM
22/04/25	24	3:09:40 AM	22/04/25	24	3:36:06 AM
23/04/25	25	3:42:39 AM	23/04/25	25	4:00:58 AM
24/04/25	26	4:13:38 AM	24/04/25	26	4:23:04 AM
25/04/25	27	4:44:04 AM	25/04/25	27	4:44:01 AM
26/04/25	28	5:15:31 AM	26/04/25	28	5:05:24 AM
27/04/25	29	5:49:41 AM	27/04/25	29	5:28:56 AM
27/04/25	1	3:33:22 PM	27/04/25	1	8:33:22 PM
28/04/25	2	6:28:26 AM	28/04/25	2	5:56:45 AM
29/04/25	3	7:13:30 AM	29/04/25	3	6:31:25 AM
30/04/25	4	8:05:56 AM	30/04/25	4	7:15:41 AM

You can find the description of each lunar day in the chapter "A Guide to The Moon Cycle and Lunar Days"

April is a time of changes in your personal life. However, financial matters cannot be ignored either. Remember, it's important to balance work and personal life.

Business. Professionally active Pisceans will dedicate April to resolving old disputes with partners. This could involve real estate or other major assets. Additionally, the month, especially its second half, is suitable for negotiations with distant colleagues and investors.

However, in the first half of April, affairs and negotiations may be prolonged, and you must come to terms with this. Demonstrating impatience and dissatisfaction will yield no results and won't improve your position. Mercury and Venus are retrograde from March 2 to April 13, making delays inevitable. But this is a good time to identify and correct errors in your work.

In the second half of April or in May, the work you've done will undoubtedly bear fruit. During this period, a trip or preparation for one is also possible. Those staying home can negotiate with former partners from distant places and restore previously lost connections.

Money. Financially, April is quite stable. Money will come in as usual, and in addition to official income, you can expect additional profits. Some will receive help from parents or a close person, while others may gain money from successful real estate transactions.

Love and Family. In many cases, the main events of April will occur in your personal life. Parents will have the opportunity to focus closely on their children's affairs, and they will bring some joy. Meetings with children living in another city or country are possible. Many Pisceans may change their place of residence — some to a new home, others to another city or country. In some cases, a return to a previous residence is planned.

Many families may welcome new children or grandchildren. Relationships for lovers may stabilize after some hesitation and doubts. There will be a realization that "an old friend is better than two new ones," and the decision to renew relationships or possibly take them to a new level will likely be mutual.

Health. In April, your energy levels are somewhat weakened, but by leading a healthy lifestyle, you can avoid troubles. The last ten days of the month are challenging, conflict-prone, and injury-prone. During this period, be more cautious in contacts, and attentive while traveling and driving.

May

New York Time			London Time		
Calendar Day	Lunar Day	Lunar Day Start Time	Calendar Day	Lunar Day	Lunar Day Start Time
01/05/25	5	9:05:19 AM	01/05/25	5	8:11:11 AM
02/05/25	6	10:09:26 AM	02/05/25	6	9:16:40 AM
03/05/25	7	11:15:16 AM	03/05/25	7	10:28:08 AM
04/05/25	8	12:20:22 PM	04/05/25	8	11:41:15 AM
05/05/25	9	1:23:31 PM	05/05/25	9	12:53:14 PM
06/05/25	10	2:24:30 PM	06/05/25	10	2:03:05 PM
07/05/25	11	3:23:48 PM	07/05/25	11	3:11:00 PM
08/05/25	12	4:22:07 PM	08/05/25	12	4:17:39 PM
09/05/25	13	5:20:12 PM	09/05/25	13	5:23:51 PM
10/05/25	14	6:18:36 PM	10/05/25	14	6:30:15 PM
11/05/25	15	7:17:32 PM	11/05/25	15	7:37:03 PM
12/05/25	16	8:16:41 PM	12/05/25	16	8:43:42 PM
13/05/25	17	9:15:07 PM	13/05/25	17	9:48:45 PM
14/05/25	18	10:11:20 PM	14/05/25	18	10:49:50 PM
15/05/25	19	11:03:44 PM	15/05/25	19	11:44:18 PM
16/05/25	20	11:51:04 PM	17/05/25	20	12:30:30 AM
18/05/25	21	12:32:59 AM	18/05/25	21	1:08:20 AM
19/05/25	22	1:09:56 AM	19/05/25	22	1:39:05 AM
20/05/25	23	1:43:01 AM	20/05/25	23	2:04:37 AM
21/05/25	24	2:13:30 AM	21/05/25	24	2:26:46 AM
22/05/25	25	2:42:50 AM	22/05/25	25	2:47:10 AM
23/05/25	26	3:12:29 AM	23/05/25	26	3:07:20 AM
24/05/25	27	3:44:07 AM	24/05/25	27	3:28:51 AM
25/05/25	28	4:19:32 AM	25/05/25	28	3:53:37 AM
26/05/25	29	5:00:45 AM	26/05/25	29	4:24:00 AM
26/05/25	1	11:04:26 PM	27/05/25	1	4:04:26 AM
27/05/25	2	5:49:31 AM	27/05/25	2	5:03:00 AM
28/05/25	3	6:46:27 AM	28/05/25	3	5:53:21 AM
29/05/25	4	7:50:12 AM	29/05/25	4	6:55:42 AM
30/05/25	5	8:57:40 AM	30/05/25	5	8:07:03 AM
31/05/25	6	10:05:27 AM	31/05/25	6	9:22:16 AM

You can find the description of each lunar day in the chapter "A Guide to The Moon Cycle and Lunar Days"

An energetic and highly productive period lies ahead. Bravely flap your fins, and the current will carry you right where you need to be!

Business. May is exceptionally favorable in the professional realm. You will excel at quickly resolving emerging issues without making mistakes, a highly valuable skill.

Connections with colleagues from other cities or countries will flourish, with successful negotiations and potential travel opportunities.

May particularly favors creative projects and unconventional solutions. However, practical matters will also be handled successfully.

Entrepreneurs and managers will complete work related to business expansion, involving construction or large-scale renovations. In all endeavors this month, managers can confidently rely on their subordinates, and employees can depend on their colleagues. There will be plenty of work for all Pisces, but the benefits will be substantial.

Complex relationships with partners concerning real estate are approaching a favorable resolution. Many issues will be resolved through financial means or other material assets.

Money. May is quite good financially. Money will flow in regularly, with noticeable increases.

Many Pisces will earn additional profits from significant work done in previous months and in May.

Additionally, there are potential earnings from successful real estate transactions. The estimated dates for the largest sums are May 4, 5, 14, 15, 23, 24, and 31.

Love and Family. Personal life this month may be just as important as work. Most Pisces will continue improving their homes, and this busy process is nearing completion. Old disputes related to real estate, especially for divorced or divorcing couples, are also coming to an end.

Relationships with relatives will significantly improve, with potential trips and meetings with family living in other cities or countries.

Many Pisces will head to distant lands, warm seas, and sunny places, or, in a more modest version, to their cottages. However, staying home will not be an option for anyone.

Health. This month, you are in excellent shape, and all ailments will steer clear of you. May is a great time for sports, shopping, and a complete makeover, so choose what suits you best.

June

New York Time			London Time		
Calendar Day	Lunar Day	Lunar Day Start Time	Calendar Day	Lunar Day	Lunar Day Start Time
01/06/25	7	11:11:20 AM	01/06/25	7	10:37:07 AM
02/06/25	8	12:14:34 PM	02/06/25	8	11:49:35 AM
03/06/25	9	1:15:23 PM	03/06/25	9	12:59:22 PM
04/06/25	10	2:14:30 PM	04/06/25	10	2:07:05 PM
05/06/25	11	3:12:49 PM	05/06/25	11	3:13:41 PM
06/06/25	12	4:11:06 PM	06/06/25	12	4:20:02 PM
07/06/25	13	5:09:50 PM	07/06/25	13	5:26:41 PM
08/06/25	14	6:09:02 PM	08/06/25	14	6:33:32 PM
09/06/25	15	7:08:03 PM	09/06/25	15	7:39:34 PM
10/06/25	16	8:05:35 PM	10/06/25	16	8:42:39 PM
11/06/25	17	8:59:53 PM	11/06/25	17	9:40:03 PM
12/06/25	18	9:49:24 PM	12/06/25	18	10:29:28 PM
13/06/25	19	10:33:21 PM	13/06/25	19	11:10:10 PM
14/06/25	20	11:11:52 PM	14/06/25	20	11:43:04 PM
15/06/25	21	11:45:53 PM	16/06/25	21	12:09:56 AM
17/06/25	22	12:16:39 AM	17/06/25	22	12:32:42 AM
18/06/25	23	12:45:34 AM	18/06/25	23	12:53:04 AM
19/06/25	24	1:14:04 AM	19/06/25	24	1:12:33 AM
20/06/25	25	1:43:40 AM	20/06/25	25	1:32:38 AM
21/06/25	26	2:16:06 AM	21/06/25	26	1:54:57 AM
22/06/25	27	2:53:14 AM	22/06/25	27	2:21:35 AM
23/06/25	28	3:37:06 AM	23/06/25	28	2:55:14 AM
24/06/25	29	4:29:11 AM	24/06/25	29	3:38:58 AM
25/06/25	30	5:29:32 AM	25/06/25	30	4:35:02 AM
25/06/25	1	6:33:30 AM	25/06/25	1	11:33:30 AM
26/06/25	2	6:35:58 AM	26/06/25	2	5:42:42 AM
27/06/25	3	7:45:00 AM	27/06/25	3	6:57:38 AM
28/06/25	4	8:53:25 AM	28/06/25	4	8:14:36 AM
29/06/25	5	9:59:26 AM	29/06/25	5	9:30:03 AM
30/06/25	6	11:02:39 AM	30/06/25	6	10:42:38 AM

You can find the description of each lunar day in the chapter "A Guide to The Moon Cycle and Lunar Days"

The pace of this month may be quite slow. As the saying goes, "Slow and steady wins the race," and it seems particularly fitting for you now.

Business. For most entrepreneurs and managers, the primary task will be completing projects related to business expansion. This likely involves construction and various administrative activities that may have occupied you for an entire year. Now it's time to finish what you started and evaluate the results. The only downside is the cost. Many of you may need to part with a significant sum in mid-month, indicating that completing your plans might require more funds than initially expected.

Employees might find themselves torn between home and work, and personal matters could take precedence. It might be wise to consider taking a vacation or a few days off – opportunities for this will certainly arise.

Many Pisces may face issues with colleagues from other cities or countries, with the most challenging period being from June 14th to 20th. These misunderstandings will eventually be resolved, but for now, be patient and tackle the most difficult issues. The root of these problems might be the inappropriate behavior of subordinates or colleagues, so keep a close eye on things and remember the saying: "A chain is only as strong as its weakest link."

Money. June's financial situation is characterized by conflicting trends. Money will come in and go out, but by the end of the month, your financial balance may be negative. The largest expenses will occur from June 14th to 19th, due to both business and personal matters.

Love and Family. For many Pisces, the main events in June will happen at home and with family. Loyal couples and committed lovers may invest time and money into creating their cozy nest. Fortunately, these demanding activities are coming to an end. Disagreements over home improvements may arise frequently, but the most challenging time will be mid-month, from June 14th to 20th. During this period, financial issues may come to light, and your partner may have their own perspective on the events. Additionally, many families may face problems with children, leading to significant expenses.

Another potential issue in June could be conflicts with relatives. This is not a new problem, but an old issue resurfacing in a new way.

Health. In June, your energy levels will be low, and the stars strongly recommend that you take care of yourself and practice moderation in all things. Be particularly cautious during travel and while driving throughout the month, especially from June 14th to 20th.

July

New York Time			London Time		
Calendar Day	Lunar Day	Lunar Day Start Time	Calendar Day	Lunar Day	Lunar Day Start Time
01/07/25	7	12:03:31 PM	01/07/25	7	11:52:30 AM
02/07/25	8	1:02:51 PM	02/07/25	8	1:00:25 PM
03/07/25	9	2:01:32 PM	03/07/25	9	2:07:23 PM
04/07/25	10	3:00:14 PM	04/07/25	10	3:14:08 PM
05/07/25	11	3:59:17 PM	05/07/25	11	4:21:00 PM
06/07/25	12	4:58:27 PM	06/07/25	12	5:27:28 PM
07/07/25	13	5:56:47 PM	07/07/25	13	6:31:59 PM
08/07/25	14	6:52:43 PM	08/07/25	14	7:32:01 PM
09/07/25	15	7:44:34 PM	09/07/25	15	8:24:58 PM
10/07/25	16	8:31:07 PM	10/07/25	16	9:09:17 PM
11/07/25	17	9:12:04 PM	11/07/25	17	9:45:15 PM
12/07/25	18	9:48:01 PM	12/07/25	18	10:14:23 PM
13/07/25	19	10:20:06 PM	13/07/25	19	10:38:37 PM
14/07/25	20	10:49:40 PM	14/07/25	20	10:59:46 PM
15/07/25	21	11:18:08 PM	15/07/25	21	11:19:24 PM
16/07/25	22	11:46:57 PM	16/07/25	22	11:38:58 PM
18/07/25	23	12:17:41 AM	18/07/25	23	12:00:00 AM
19/07/25	24	12:52:03 AM	19/07/25	24	12:24:17 AM
20/07/25	25	1:31:59 AM	20/07/25	25	12:54:07 AM
21/07/25	26	2:19:12 AM	21/07/25	26	1:32:20 AM
22/07/25	27	3:14:38 AM	22/07/25	27	2:21:42 AM
23/07/25	28	4:17:24 AM	23/07/25	28	3:23:11 AM
24/07/25	29	5:24:52 AM	24/07/25	29	4:34:26 AM
24/07/25	1	3:12:27 PM	24/07/25	1	8:12:27 PM
25/07/25	2	6:33:41 AM	25/07/25	2	5:50:39 AM
26/07/25	3	7:41:19 AM	26/07/25	3	7:07:24 AM
27/07/25	4	8:46:34 AM	27/07/25	4	8:22:10 AM
28/07/25	5	9:49:20 AM	28/07/25	5	9:34:13 AM
29/07/25	6	10:50:08 AM	29/07/25	6	10:43:56 AM
30/07/25	7	11:49:44 AM	30/07/25	7	11:52:04 AM
31/07/25	8	12:48:49 PM	31/07/25	8	12:59:26 PM

You can find the description of each lunar day in the chapter "A Guide to The Moon Cycle and Lunar Days"

July is looking quite positive for you. You will be able to handle a variety of tasks, showcase your wit, and become the star of any party. So, go ahead with confidence!

Business. July is more suited for rest and attending to personal and family matters, while work can wait. However, for those who can't resist work or have obligations that keep them at the office, you'll still be able to make contributions this month Entrepreneurs will wrap up important activities related to business expansion, possibly involving major construction or other real estate operations. Employees can calmly handle their current tasks, but the stars suggest that your thoughts might be elsewhere. So, consider taking a break, especially since opportunities for rest will arise this month.

July is an excellent time for people in creative professions—your popularity will increase, and so will your earnings. The best time for all professional matters is the first half of the month. In the second half, Mercury goes retrograde, causing significant slowdowns in all affairs. For you, this is a good chance to evaluate what's happening and calmly finish what you've already started.

Money. The financial situation is modest There won't be a lot of money this month, but support from close people, parents, or a spouse might come through. There will also be chances to secure a favorable loan.

Love and Family. Your personal life will be vibrant this month. Home improvement projects are coming to an end, and there are still many plans related to developing existing relationships. This could mean the birth of children or plans related to pregnancy.

Those who are still single may meet someone special and start an exciting romance. Parents will be pleased with their children's achievements, and the atmosphere in most families will be warm and festive.

Additionally, July will be full of parties and various festive events. Some complications in relationships between spouses and lovers could arise in the last ten days of the month, but the situation will quickly resolve.

Health. This month, you are healthy, energetic, successful, and efficient in solving any tasks. July is a great time for shopping, self-improvement, and any cosmetic procedures.

August

New York Time			London Time		
Calendar Day	Lunar Day	Lunar Day Start Time	Calendar Day	Lunar Day	Lunar Day Start Time
01/08/25	9	1:47:52 PM	01/08/25	9	2:06:29 PM
02/08/25	10	2:46:56 PM	02/08/25	10	3:13:09 PM
03/08/25	11	3:45:28 PM	03/08/25	11	4:18:25 PM
04/08/25	12	4:42:18 PM	04/08/25	12	5:20:17 PM
05/08/25	13	5:35:51 PM	05/08/25	13	6:16:13 PM
06/08/25	14	6:24:46 PM	06/08/25	14	7:04:12 PM
07/08/25	15	7:08:18 PM	07/08/25	15	7:43:44 PM
08/08/25	16	7:46:41 PM	08/08/25	16	8:15:49 PM
09/08/25	17	8:20:47 PM	09/08/25	17	8:42:14 PM
10/08/25	18	8:51:51 PM	10/08/25	18	9:04:52 PM
11/08/25	19	9:21:14 PM	11/08/25	19	9:25:23 PM
12/08/25	20	9:50:23 PM	12/08/25	20	9:45:16 PM
13/08/25	21	10:20:46 PM	13/08/25	21	10:06:00 PM
14/08/25	22	10:53:59 PM	14/08/25	22	10:29:15 PM
15/08/25	23	11:31:48 PM	15/08/25	23	10:57:01 PM
17/08/25	24	12:15:55 AM	16/08/25	24	11:31:51 PM
18/08/25	25	1:07:28 AM	18/08/25	25	12:16:25 AM
19/08/25	26	2:06:21 AM	19/08/25	26	1:12:23 AM
20/08/25	27	3:10:47 AM	20/08/25	27	2:18:46 AM
21/08/25	28	4:17:57 AM	21/08/25	28	3:31:58 AM
22/08/25	29	5:25:15 AM	22/08/25	29	4:47:37 AM
23/08/25	1	2:07:07 AM	23/08/25	30	6:02:39 AM
23/08/25	2	6:31:03 AM	23/08/25	1	7:07:07 AM
24/08/25	3	7:34:46 AM	24/08/25	2	7:15:41 AM
25/08/25	4	8:36:36 AM	25/08/25	3	8:26:33 AM
26/08/25	5	9:37:03 AM	26/08/25	4	9:35:44 AM
27/08/25	6	10:36:42 AM	27/08/25	5	10:43:51 AM
28/08/25	7	11:36:02 AM	28/08/25	6	11:51:23 AM
29/08/25	8	12:35:09 PM	29/08/25	7	12:58:21 PM
30/08/25	9	1:33:43 PM	30/08/25	8	2:04:07 PM
31/08/25	10	2:30:52 PM	31/08/25	9	3:07:07 PM

You can find the description of each lunar day in the chapter "A Guide to The Moon Cycle and Lunar Days"

August is a challenging month; it will present a variety of tasks, each requiring your attention and participation. The advice is simple—don't try to chase too many goals at once, or you might end up with nothing.

Business. In the first third of the month, you may encounter delays and problems. Entrepreneurs and managers might face misunderstandings with subordinates who won't show their best side. Remember, your careful management can prevent many issues, so be proactive.

Employees may experience misunderstandings with colleagues and workplace intrigues, which are best ignored. Financial demands from partners or colleagues are also likely in the first ten days of August, which you will need to address.

From August 10th onwards, the periods are calmer and potentially more productive. Those dealing with complex real estate issues will complete one challenging phase and can move on to the next, which looks innovative and interesting, though it will require significant resources. However, most of you are creative individuals, so things will go well in this area.

Money. Your financial situation is modest but stable. Besides regular earnings, you can expect pleasant surprises such as gifts, bonuses, or even a lottery win. You can also rely on strong support from close people. Major expenses are likely from August 7th to 10th and may be related to work or personal life, household, and family needs.

Love and Family. Personal life is generally calm, especially from August 10th onwards. The first 10 days of the month are challenging for both lovers and spouses, with likely misunderstandings, confusion, and household problems. After August 10th, things will stabilize, and everything will run more smoothly.

August will bring many interesting events related to children, and in the second half of the month, it will become clear that the older ones are thriving and the younger ones are behaving well and admirably. Your children might even demonstrate a unique and rare talent. Many families may welcome new children or grandchildren.

For lovers, the period from August 10th to 20th is also a great time. If you already have a close person, the relationship will significantly improve, and if not, the chance of meeting someone special is quite high. Those engaged in various real estate transactions can complete one stage and move on to the next, which might involve home decoration, buying furniture, and other necessary household items.

Health. In August, your energy levels are not high, but no serious problems are expected, especially if you maintain a healthy diet and remember the benefits of good sleep.

September

New York Time			London Time		
Calendar Day	Lunar Day	Lunar Day Start Time	Calendar Day	Lunar Day	Lunar Day Start Time
01/09/25	11	3:25:18 PM	01/09/25	10	4:05:09 PM
02/09/25	12	4:15:42 PM	02/09/25	11	4:56:04 PM
03/09/25	13	5:01:10 PM	03/09/25	12	5:38:50 PM
04/09/25	14	5:41:37 PM	04/09/25	13	6:13:52 PM
05/09/25	15	6:17:37 PM	05/09/25	14	6:42:41 PM
06/09/25	16	6:50:16 PM	06/09/25	15	7:07:04 PM
07/09/25	17	7:20:51 PM	07/09/25	16	7:28:45 PM
08/09/25	18	7:50:45 PM	08/09/25	17	7:49:18 PM
09/09/25	19	8:21:26 PM	09/09/25	18	8:10:12 PM
10/09/25	20	8:54:28 PM	10/09/25	19	8:33:04 PM
11/09/25	21	9:31:31 PM	11/09/25	20	8:59:48 PM
12/09/25	22	10:14:16 PM	12/09/25	21	9:32:46 PM
13/09/25	23	11:03:55 PM	13/09/25	22	10:14:33 PM
15/09/25	24	12:00:35 AM	14/09/25	23	11:07:04 PM
16/09/25	25	1:02:54 AM	16/09/25	24	12:09:59 AM
17/09/25	26	2:08:23 AM	17/09/25	25	1:20:23 AM
18/09/25	27	3:14:35 AM	18/09/25	26	2:34:13 AM
19/09/25	28	4:19:47 AM	19/09/25	27	3:48:17 AM
20/09/25	29	5:23:20 AM	20/09/25	28	5:00:57 AM
21/09/25	30	6:25:13 AM	21/09/25	29	6:11:49 AM
21/09/25	1	3:54:37 PM	21/09/25	1	8:54:37 PM
22/09/25	2	7:25:51 AM	22/09/25	2	7:21:12 AM
23/09/25	3	8:25:44 AM	23/09/25	3	8:29:36 AM
24/09/25	4	9:25:17 AM	24/09/25	4	9:37:27 AM
25/09/25	5	10:24:36 AM	25/09/25	5	10:44:49 AM
26/09/25	6	11:23:24 AM	26/09/25	6	11:51:09 AM
27/09/25	7	12:20:54 PM	27/09/25	7	12:55:09 PM
28/09/25	8	1:15:55 PM	28/09/25	8	1:54:47 PM
29/09/25	9	2:07:12 PM	29/09/25	9	2:47:56 PM
30/09/25	10	2:53:49 PM	30/09/25	10	3:33:14 PM

You can find the description of each lunar day in the chapter "A Guide to The Moon Cycle and Lunar Days"

September promises to be festive and romantic. If you have any energy left for work, you'll have ample opportunities to shine.

Business. Expect a dynamic work period ahead. Partnerships are crucial, and you'll witness an interesting phenomenon: old connections will fade away, making room for new ones. Your task during this period is to part ways with former colleagues gracefully and build strong relationships with new ones. This will require wisdom, tact, and flexibility to navigate the challenges that may arise. The stars are confident that you will succeed!

The last third part of September will be the most challenging for relationships with former partners. Creative professionals—actors, artists, musicians, and writers—can expect particular success. Opportunities to showcase your talents to a broader audience and increase your income will arise. In fact, all Pisces will have the chance to present their achievements and gain recognition among peers. Just make sure you have something valuable to offer.

Money. September will be financially turbulent. Significant income is possible in the first half of the month, while substantial expenses are likely in the last 10 days of the month.

Love and Family. For many Pisces, personal life will take precedence over work and career. New relationships will form easily and develop quickly. This is great for singles but may cause problems for those who already have a partner. Remember, making a choice isn't always easy or pleasant and can be challenging and even painful. Keep this in mind and analyze the situation carefully before crossing any "red lines."

Parents will be delighted by their children, and many Pisces are planning to expand their families. Significant sums may periodically be allocated from the family budget for the needs of the younger generation.

Health. Your energy levels will be high for most of the month. However, you'll likely feel tired in the last days of September from all the social events and gatherings. While these activities enhance life, they can also make you yearn for solitude. Listen to your body, and if you feel fatigued, take the time to rest.

October

New York Time		
Calendar Day	Lunar Day	Lunar Day Start Time
01/10/25	11	3:35:29 PM
02/10/25	12	4:12:39 PM
03/10/25	13	4:46:13 PM
04/10/25	14	5:17:26 PM
05/10/25	15	5:47:36 PM
06/10/25	16	6:18:12 PM
07/10/25	17	6:50:46 PM
08/10/25	18	7:27:02 PM
09/10/25	19	8:08:48 PM
10/10/25	20	8:57:29 PM
11/10/25	21	9:53:27 PM
12/10/25	22	10:55:30 PM
14/10/25	23	12:01:01 AM
15/10/25	24	1:07:18 AM
16/10/25	25	2:12:31 AM
17/10/25	26	3:15:53 AM
18/10/25	27	4:17:28 AM
19/10/25	28	5:17:46 AM
20/10/25	29	6:17:21 AM
21/10/25	30	7:16:43 AM
21/10/25	1	8:25:59 AM
22/10/25	2	8:16:03 AM
23/10/25	3	9:15:08 AM
24/10/25	4	10:13:13 AM
25/10/25	5	11:09:06 AM
26/10/25	6	11:01:25 AM
27/10/25	7	11:49:05 AM
28/10/25	8	12:31:40 PM
29/10/25	9	1:09:27 PM
30/10/25	10	1:43:19 PM
31/10/25	11	2:14:24 PM

London Time		
Calendar Day	Lunar Day	Lunar Day Start Time
01/10/25	11	4:10:41 PM
02/10/25	12	4:41:28 PM
03/10/25	13	5:07:18 PM
04/10/25	14	5:29:54 PM
05/10/25	15	5:50:52 PM
06/10/25	16	6:11:41 PM
07/10/25	17	6:33:58 PM
08/10/25	18	6:59:32 PM
09/10/25	19	7:30:45 PM
10/10/25	20	8:10:17 PM
11/10/25	21	9:00:28 PM
12/10/25	22	10:01:37 PM
13/10/25	23	11:11:03 PM
15/10/25	24	12:24:30 AM
16/10/25	25	1:38:22 AM
17/10/25	26	2:50:47 AM
18/10/25	27	4:01:20 AM
19/10/25	28	5:10:19 AM
20/10/25	29	6:18:22 AM
21/10/25	30	7:26:00 AM
21/10/25	1	1:25:59 PM
22/10/25	2	8:33:27 AM
23/10/25	3	9:40:18 AM
24/10/25	4	10:45:21 AM
25/10/25	5	11:46:38 AM
26/10/25	6	11:41:55 AM
27/10/25	7	12:29:30 PM
28/10/25	8	1:09:01 PM
29/10/25	9	1:41:23 PM
30/10/25	10	2:08:14 PM
31/10/25	11	2:31:18 PM

You can find the description of each lunar day in the chapter "A Guide to The Moon Cycle and Lunar Days"

The upcoming month looks wonderful, though it might be financially draining. You are in demand and popular, and now you need to figure out how to use these qualities to your advantage.

Business. For most of you, the main events in October will occur in your personal life. Exceptions include the ever-busy workaholics and all those in creative professions: actors, singers, artists, musicians, and anyone whose work involves words. Even if you don't fall into these categories but have a desire to showcase your talents to a select group of colleagues or the general public, nothing will stop you from doing so.

Connections with colleagues from other cities or countries are significant, with the potential to renew relationships with old colleagues and distant friends. The second half of the month is the best time for professional endeavors. The first half isn't unsuccessful; it just requires more effort to achieve your goals.

Money. Your financial position in October is unstable, which is perhaps the only downside this month. Money will be spent continuously, primarily on personal life, leisure, and the needs of loved ones. And let's not forget shopping.

Love and Family. Personal life may take precedence over professional duties this month. Various but equally interesting developments are in store. Recent romances are progressing well, with relationships becoming more serious, deeper, and more stable. Even any disagreements likely in October can be summed up by the saying, "lovers' tiffs are harmless."

Families will be heavily involved in the affairs of their children, with significant investments in their upbringing, education, and development. Many families might welcome new children or grandchildren, or start planning for this important event. Many of you will continue home improvement projects, investing nerves, money, and time into these efforts.

There will also be time for rest in October. Both spouses and lovers might take a trip, with probable dates being the second half of October and the first half of November.

Health. Your energy levels are low in October, so protect yourself from winter colds and infections. Remember the benefits of maintaining a healthy lifestyle.

November

New York Time		
Calendar Day	Lunar Day	Lunar Day Start Time
01/11/25	12	2:44:02 PM
02/11/25	13	3:13:35 PM
03/11/25	14	3:44:37 PM
04/11/25	15	4:18:51 PM
05/11/25	16	4:58:15 PM
06/11/25	17	5:44:43 PM
07/11/25	18	6:39:20 PM
08/11/25	19	7:41:29 PM
09/11/25	20	8:48:28 PM
10/11/25	21	9:56:52 PM
11/11/25	22	11:04:03 PM
13/11/25	23	12:08:51 AM
14/11/25	24	1:11:12 AM
15/11/25	25	2:11:41 AM
16/11/25	26	3:11:05 AM
17/11/25	27	4:10:05 AM
18/11/25	28	5:09:08 AM
19/11/25	29	6:08:14 AM
20/11/25	1	1:48:17 AM
20/11/25	2	7:06:48 AM
21/11/25	3	8:03:43 AM
22/11/25	4	8:57:28 AM
23/11/25	5	9:46:43 AM
24/11/25	6	10:30:42 AM
25/11/25	7	11:09:30 AM
26/11/25	8	11:43:51 AM
27/11/25	9	12:14:50 PM
28/11/25	10	12:43:46 PM
29/11/25	11	1:11:58 PM
30/11/25	12	1:40:54 PM

London Time		
Calendar Day	Lunar Day	Lunar Day Start Time
01/11/25	12	2:52:11 PM
02/11/25	13	3:12:24 PM
03/11/25	14	3:33:26 PM
04/11/25	15	3:57:02 PM
05/11/25	16	4:25:24 PM
06/11/25	17	5:01:22 PM
07/11/25	18	5:47:56 PM
08/11/25	19	6:46:43 PM
09/11/25	20	7:55:56 PM
10/11/25	21	9:10:50 PM
11/11/25	22	10:26:42 PM
12/11/25	23	11:40:47 PM
14/11/25	24	12:52:18 AM
15/11/25	25	2:01:37 AM
16/11/25	26	3:09:31 AM
17/11/25	27	4:16:48 AM
18/11/25	28	5:23:57 AM
19/11/25	29	6:30:54 AM
20/11/25	1	6:48:17 AM
20/11/25	2	7:36:45 AM
21/11/25	3	8:39:41 AM
22/11/25	4	9:37:19 AM
23/11/25	5	10:27:32 AM
24/11/25	6	11:09:26 AM
25/11/25	7	11:43:36 AM
26/11/25	8	12:11:34 PM
27/11/25	9	12:35:06 PM
28/11/25	10	12:55:52 PM
29/11/25	11	1:15:19 PM
30/11/25	12	1:34:55 PM

You can find the description of each lunar day in the chapter "A Guide to The Moon Cycle and Lunar Days"

This month, many of you might feel as though you've grown wings. Staying in one place will be challenging, and the more energy you expend, the more it seems to replenish. The laws of physics don't seem to apply to you!

Business. In November, the main focus for most of you will be developing connections with partners from other cities or countries. A trip might be on the horizon, where you can combine business with pleasure: productive work and a lot of positive emotions. Relationships with former colleagues are being rekindled, leading to extensive discussions on important matters, ultimately resulting in a decision that satisfies both parties.

Despite the positive outlook for November, challenges still exist. While you'll find common ground with some colleagues from other cities or countries, issues may arise with others. Difficult matters may reach resolution during the Full Moon on November 5-7 or the New Moon on November 18-20. These are challenging times, but as the saying goes, "truth springs from arguments." This might just be one of those times.

Money. The financial situation is stable, and in addition to regular earnings, pleasant surprises such as bonuses or gifts from loved ones are possible. November's expenses might also be enjoyable—trips, meeting friends, spending on children, and of course, some shopping.

Love and Family. Your personal life this month looks just as exciting as your work and career. Both couples and lovers may take a trip and have a wonderful time. Meetings with old friends and relatives from other cities or countries are likely.

Parents will be able to spend more time with their children, with possible joint trips or visits to children living far away.

One of November's challenges could be dealing with family relations. An unexpected quarrel might flare up among relatives, and you may find yourself trying to reconcile conflicting interests within your family. Pay special attention during the Full Moon on November 5-7 and the New Moon on November 18-20.

Health. In November, you are healthy, energetic, and able to make a strong impression on everyone you meet. However, throughout the month, the stars recommend being extra cautious during travel and while driving.

December

New York Time		
Calendar Day	Lunar Day	Lunar Day Start Time
01/12/25	13	2:12:11 PM
02/12/25	14	2:47:45 PM
03/12/25	15	3:29:44 PM
04/12/25	16	4:20:06 PM
05/12/25	17	5:19:33 PM
06/12/25	18	6:26:30 PM
07/12/25	19	7:37:13 PM
08/12/25	20	8:47:52 PM
09/12/25	21	9:56:06 PM
10/12/25	22	11:01:11 PM
12/12/25	23	12:03:30 AM
13/12/25	24	1:03:53 AM
14/12/25	25	2:03:13 AM
15/12/25	26	3:02:12 AM
16/12/25	27	4:01:11 AM
17/12/25	28	4:59:56 AM
18/12/25	29	5:57:36 AM
19/12/25	30	6:52:47 AM
19/12/25	1	8:44:26 PM
20/12/25	2	7:43:58 AM
21/12/25	3	8:30:02 AM
22/12/25	4	9:10:41 AM
23/12/25	5	9:46:23 AM
24/12/25	6	10:18:08 AM
25/12/25	7	10:47:09 AM
26/12/25	8	11:14:44 AM
27/12/25	9	11:42:15 AM
28/12/25	10	12:11:11 PM
29/12/25	11	12:43:13 PM
30/12/25	12	1:20:22 PM
31/12/25	13	2:04:48 PM

London Time		
Calendar Day	Lunar Day	Lunar Day Start Time
01/12/25	13	1:56:10 PM
02/12/25	14	2:21:02 PM
03/12/25	15	2:52:03 PM
04/12/25	16	3:32:32 PM
05/12/25	17	4:25:33 PM
06/12/25	18	5:31:38 PM
07/12/25	19	6:47:06 PM
08/12/25	20	8:06:01 PM
09/12/25	21	9:23:50 PM
10/12/25	22	10:38:35 PM
11/12/25	23	11:50:11 PM
13/12/25	24	12:59:23 AM
14/12/25	25	2:07:11 AM
15/12/25	26	3:14:23 AM
16/12/25	27	4:21:19 AM
17/12/25	28	5:27:33 AM
18/12/25	29	6:31:44 AM
19/12/25	30	7:31:36 AM
20/12/25	1	1:44:26 AM
20/12/25	2	8:24:45 AM
21/12/25	3	9:09:40 AM
22/12/25	4	9:46:24 AM
23/12/25	5	10:16:12 AM
24/12/25	6	10:40:50 AM
25/12/25	7	11:02:01 AM
26/12/25	8	11:21:17 AM
27/12/25	9	11:40:00 AM
28/12/25	10	11:59:34 AM
29/12/25	11	12:21:37 PM
30/12/25	12	12:48:15 PM
31/12/25	13	1:22:22 PM

You can find the description of each lunar day in the chapter "A Guide to The Moon Cycle and Lunar Days"

In December, your energy levels may be off the charts. If you can channel it in the right direction, you'll achieve a lot. The stars will be especially favorable to those whose work requires precision and a creative approach. This is your moment to shine!

Business. The major successes in December can be achieved on the professional front. Ongoing projects will wrap up successfully, and new opportunities will emerge.

For entrepreneurs and managers, this means new plans that could receive approval at the highest level. Employees have a good chance of earning their boss's approval, getting a promotion, or securing a position in a more promising organization. There are many opportunities, and it's up to you to seize them.

You might lack some flexibility and understanding of the significance of what's happening right now. So, before making any decisions—whether to reject an offer or accept it—consider all options and possibilities carefully, and the stars will surely support you.

Money. Financially, this month is excellent. Money will flow in steadily, and the amount will significantly increase. In addition to your usual income, bonuses, rewards, and gifts from loved ones are also likely.

Expected dates for large sums are December 1, 8-10, 19, 20, and 27-29. Expenses are few, and all will be offset by growing income.

Love and Family. Your personal life takes a back seat to work in December. Lovers may not get to meet as often as they would like, which could strain relationships.

Supportive spouses will understand and back each other up. The stars remind you that a smile and a kind word can ease tension even in the toughest situations. Also, in matters of personal relationships, trust your intuition—it's likely to guide you well.

Health. Your energy levels are through the roof in December. Surprisingly, the more you expend, the more you'll have. With such an abundance of energy, all illnesses will steer clear of you.

Pisces Description

Sign. Feminine, water, mutable.

Ruler. Neptune, Pluto.

Exaltation. Venus.

Positive traits. Highly imaginative, kind, adaptable, tranquil, peaceful, receptive, impressive, modest, compassionate, caring, delicate, gentle, idealistic, religious, deep.

Negative traits. Passive, shy, fanatical, impractical, fantastical, slovenly, volatile, unreliable, self-indulgent, overly sensual, malleable, submissive, dependent, moody, lazy, apathetic.

Weaknesses in the body. Legs – ankles, toe joints, toes. Tendons and ligaments. Digestive, lymphatic, and endocrine systems, heart and circulatory system.

Metal. Platinum and tin.

Minerals. For a talisman – amethyst and chrysolite. Opal, jasper, and coral are compatible.

Numbers. 3, 11, 19.

Day. Thursday.

Color. Purple and indigo.

Pisces energy

Pisces is influenced by the energies of both Neptune and Jupiter. In ancient cultures, Neptune was revered as the ruler of the seas. He represents the primal ocean and chaos where all opportunities lie, but nothing ever comes to life on its own. Neptune is the highest faith, psychic phenomena, hypersensitivity, deep and intuitive understanding of things and capacity for unearthly love. All of these traits are inherent to Pisces, and generous Jupiter bestows them with confidence in their own importance, a happy life, and great vitality.

Astrological portrait of Pisces

Pisces closes the Zodiac. This sign is a mirror of all the others, with a focus on their strengths and weaknesses. Pisces is a self-redeemer who is able to purify others by taking on the negativity. That is Pisces's greatest mission. Empathy, compassion, and the ability to reflect the qualities of any other sign with detachment are her main traits. "I feel, therefore I am" is Pisces's motto. However, in their negative manifestations, Pisces are ambivalent, unreliable, and prone to betrayal at any time. They make big promises and hardly ever follow through. They seek their own benefits and are very dishonest. Pisces always reflect their environment, which will determine their behavior. They are easily influenced by others, though this is usually unconscious. Without even realizing it, they take on the feelings and thoughts of whomever they are talking to. They can get carried away and simply go with the flow like water, not trying to change their own destiny. Pisces lack willpower and the ability to stand on their own two feet or have the inner core they need to resist the influence of others. Pisces is symbolized by two fish swimming in opposite directions. One fish is living, while the other is depicted as dead. This is Pisces – the living fish is in harmony with God and one with the cosmos. The dead Pisces is illusions, speculation of one's own weakness, opportunism, and chaos. At their worst, Pisces are capable of showing the vile human traits, only to be tormented by remorse afterward.

Pisces is a wise sign, with an understanding of others' suffering. They are capable of sacrificing themselves to help others. They are humane, merciful, and optimistic. But they are also overly sensitive and feel others' pain as their own. Pisces make good psychologists, and they are drawn to that which is hidden. They like to wrap their lives in mystery and express themselves symbolically. They tend to fantasize a lot. Others may not always understand Pisces, which causes her to suffer. She hates arguments and scandal but would rather tolerate evil and injustice than actually fight them. She has a good sense of humor, is friendly, humble, and calm. This draws many people in and opens doors. Pisces wants financial well-being but is rarely able to gain it on her own. As Pisces ages, she is eventually able to achieve peace and prosperity.

Pisces's great task is to carry divine love into the world, have compassion for her neighbors, and help them in their spiritual development. Nearly all Pisces are creative – many are musicians, artists, writers, performers, psychologist, or mystics.

How to recognize Pisces by appearances

Pisces is a sign that is constantly changing. Their appearance is a reflection of their inner state. Pisces tend to have large, deep, and alluring eyes, with an inward or wandering gaze that makes them look mysterious and almost absent. Pisces hardly ever look others in the eye. Their eyelids often appear red and irritated. Their skin is soft, pale, and almost transparent. Their hair is thin rather than thick, and their hands are small and soft, even in men. Pisces tend to gain weight, but they keep an eye on their figure.

Charting Pisces's Fate

Pisces's life path is often difficult and full of ups and downs. If she is not guided by someone else's strong hand, she may not achieve success. Pisces needs something or someone to stimulate and inspire her, especially among men. Female Pisces are often strong-minded, strong-willed individuals who forge their own path in life and are very successful in all of their endeavors.

A guide to the Moon cycle and Lunar days

Since Ancient times, people have noticed that the moon has a strong influence on nature. Our Earth and everything living on it is a single living being, which is why the phases of the moon have such an effect on our health and mental state, and therefore, our lives. Remember Shakespeare and his description of Othello's jealousy in his famous tragedy:

"It is the very error of the moon, She comes more nearer Earth than she was wont And makes men mad."

If our inner rhythm is in harmony with that of the cosmos, we are able to achieve much more. People were aware of this a thousand years ago. The lunar calendar is ancient. We can find it among the ancient Sumerians (4000-3000 BC), the inhabitants of Mesopotamia, Native Americans, Hindus, and ancient Slavs. There is evidence that the Siberian Yakuts had a lunar calendar, as did the Malaysians.

Primitive tribes saw the moon as a source of fertility. Long before Christianity, the waxing moon was seen as favorable for planting new crops and starting a new business, for success and making money, while the waning moon was a sign that business would end.

1 2 3 4 5 6 7 8

What are the phases of the moon?

- Phase 1 – new moon
- Phase 2 – waxing crescent moon
- Phase 3 – first quarter moon
- Phase 4 – waxing gibbous moon
- Phase 5 – full moon
- Phase 6 – waning gibbous moon
- Phase 7 – third quarter moon
- Phase 8 – waning crescent moon

To simplify things, we can divide the month into two phases:

- Waxing crescent moon - before the full moon
- Waning crescent moon - after the full moon

New moon

We cannot see the new moon, as it is hidden. People might complain about feeling weak, mental imbalance, and fatigue. During this time, we want to avoid taking on too much or overdoing things. Generally, people are not very responsive and react poorly to requests, which is why it is best to look out for yourself, while not keeping your plate too full.

The new moon is a bad time for advertising – it will go unnoticed. It is not worth preparing any presentations, parties, or loud gatherings. People are feeling constrained, not very social, and sluggish.

This is also a less than ideal time for surgery, as your recovery will be slow, and the likelihood of medical error is high.

It is also difficult to get an accurate diagnosis during the new moon – diseases might seem to be hidden, and doctors might not see the real underlying cause of what ails you.

The new moon is also a bad time for dates, and sexual encounters may be dissatisfying and leave you feeling disappointed. Ancient astrologers did not advise planning a wedding night during the new moon.

Waxing crescent moon

It is easy to identify a waxing crescent moon. If you draw an imaginary line between the two "horns", you should see the letter P. The waxing moon is then divided into one and two quarters.

During the first quarter moon, we need to focus on planning – setting goals and thinking of how we will set about achieving them. However, it is still a good idea to hold back a bit and not overdo things. Energy levels are still low, though they are growing along with the moon. It is still a good idea to avoid any medical procedures during this time.

The second quarter is a time for bold, decisive action. Things will come easy, and there is a greater chance of a lucky break. This is a good time for weddings, especially if the moon will be in Libra, Cancer, or Taurus. Nevertheless, it is a good idea to put off any advertising activities and public speaking until closer to the full moon, if you can.

Full moon

During the full moon, the Earth is located between the sun and the moon. During this time, the moon is round and fully illuminated. This takes place during days 14-16 of the lunar cycle.

During the full moon, many people feel more vigorous than usual. They are emotional, sociable, and actively seeking more contact, so this may be a good time for any celebrations.

However, be careful not to drink too much – you can relax to the point that you lose control, and the consequences of that can be very unpleasant. If you are able to stick to moderation, there is no better time for a party!

The full moon is also the best time for advertising, as not only will your campaign be widely seen, people will be apt to remember it.

The full moon is also a favorable time for dates, and during this time, people are at their most open, romantic, and willing to tell each other something important that might take their relationship to the next level of trust and understanding.

Moreover, during the full moon, people feel a surge of energy, which may lead to hyperactivity, restlessness, and insomnia.

It will be harder to keep your emotions in check. You might face conflicts with friends, disasters, and accidents. During the full moon, any surgeries are **not a good idea**, as the risk of complications and bleeding is on the rise. Plastic surgery is also a bad idea, as swelling and bruises might be much worse than in another lunar phase. At the same time, the full moon is a good time to get an accurate diagnosis.

During this time, **try to limit your calories and liquid intake** (especially if you deal with bloating and excess weight), as your body is absorbing both calories and liquids faster during the full moon, and it can be very difficult to get rid of the weight later on.

Waning crescent moon

The full moon is over, and a new phase is beginning – the waning moon. This is a quieter time, when all of the jobs you started earlier are being partly or entirely completed (it all depends on the speed and scale).

Surgery will turn out much better if it is performed during the waning moon. Your recovery will be faster, and the likelihood of complications is much lower. If you have any plans to lose weight, the waning moon is the best time to do that. This is also a good time for quitting bad habits, such as smoking or cursing.

The waning moon can also be divided into the third and fourth quarters.

Third quarter - this is a favorable period, and you are able to resolve a lot of problems without conflict. People are calming down and ready to listen and take in information, while still being active. However, this is not the best time to begin any major projects, especially if you are unsure if you will be able to complete them by the start of the new lunar month.

The third quarter is a good time to get married, especially if the moon is in Cancer, Taurus, or Libra.

Fourth quarter – This is the most passive period of the lunar cycle. You are not as strong as usual. Your energy is lagging. You will be tired until reaching a new beginning. The best thing you can do as the lunar cycle comes to an end is to get things in order, and avoid anything that might get in your way at work or in personal relationships. Examine your successes and failures.

Now, let's discuss the lunar days in greater detail. For centuries, people around the world have described the influence of lunar days, and modern astrologers only add to this work, as they compare old texts to modern life.

The 1st lunar day.

The first lunar day is extremely important for the rest of the lunar month. This is a much-needed day to carefully plan your activities and lay the groundwork for the rest of the lunar month. Remember that the first lunar day is not a good day for major activities, but rather for sitting down and planning things.

Avoid conflicts on this day, unless you want them to overshadow the rest of the month. Try to see the positive side of things and imagine that the lunar month will bring you good things both at work and in love. The more vividly you can imagine this, the sooner your desires will come to fruition. Perhaps it would be a good idea to jot down plans that will bring you closer to achieving your dreams. This is the best time for both manifesting and making wishes!

This is also a favorable day when it comes to seeking a new job or starting an academic program.

It is fine to go out on a date on the first lunar day, but limit any sexual contact, as your energy levels are low, and you are likely to end up disappointed.

Getting married on the first lunar day is not recommended.

Avoid getting a haircut – there are many indications that cutting your hair on the first lunar day will have a negative effect on your health and life expectancy.

Under no circumstances should you undergo any major cosmetic procedures, including plastic surgery. Energy levels are low, your skin is dull and almost stagnant. The results will not live up to your expectations, and in the worst-case scenario, you will end up looking worse than before. It is common for cosmetic procedures performed on this day to be disappointing or even useless. Even the best surgeons are less capable.

Your good dreams on the first lunar day foretell happiness and joy. Bad ones usually do not come true.

The 2nd lunar day.

This is considered a lucky day, and is symbolized by a cornucopia. It is not an exaggeration to say that the second lunar day is a favorable time for both work and love. It is a time for action, and a great period to work on yourself, look for a new job, start something new, or complete any financial transaction, whether a sale or purchase. This is also a great time for creative and scientific insights, and a good time for any meeting – whether political or romantic.

Any romantic dates or sexual encounters during the second lunar day are unlikely to disappoint. This is also a good day for weddings or taking a trip with someone special.

During the second lunar day, the moon is beginning its waxing phase, which is a good time for anything you might to do nourish and restore your skin. This is a great time for any cosmetic procedures aimed at preservation, though it is best to put off any plastic surgery until the waning moon. If that is not possible, then the second lunar day is acceptable, if not ideal, and you will not run into any complications.

Folklore tells us that this is not a good day for a haircut, as that may lead to arguments with a loved one.

This is the best time for exercise – your body is in good shape, and you are able to handle new exercise regimens. If the moon happens to be in Scorpio, though, be careful.

This is a good day for anything positive, but avoid any conflicts, discussions about the status of your relationship, or litigation.

Dreams of the second lunar day are usually not prophetic.

The 3rd lunar day.

On this day, we are usually able to make out a thin sliver of the lunar crescent. It is a longstanding tradition to show money during the new month – it is believed that as the moon grows, so will your savings.

However, astrological systems around the world consider this an unlucky, unfavorable day. It is not a good idea to travel, begin any new business, or give into your bad mood.

You might run into many a lot of problems at work on this day, which will cause you a lot of anxiety. However, it is a good day to take a step back and identify and set about fixing any flaws and shortcomings. Remember that everything tends to look worse on this day than it actually is.

It is not the time to ask management for anything – you are likely to walk away disappointed, and end up unfairly reprimanded rather than receiving a promotion or raise. Instead, focus on areas of work that need to be smoothed over or studied further. It will be clear what problems you are facing, and you will easily be able to find a remedy.

Do not rush to criticize your loved ones – things may not be as they appear. "Measure twice and cut once" is your motto on this day.

This is not a good day to get married, as the couple is likely to have a turbulent, short-lived marriage.

You can schedule a cosmetic procedure for this day, but only if it is relatively minor. Plastic surgery should wait.

Do exercises as usual, without overdoing it or adding any new routines.

Dreams on this day do not mean anything.

The 4th lunar day.

These are relatively neutral days, in that they are unlikely to bring anything bad, but they also will not bring you any windfalls. The fourth lunar day is symbolized by a tree of paradise, the tree of knowledge, and the choice between good and evil. Things ultimately depend on us and our final decisions.

This is a great day for anything money-related – signing contracts, agreements, or even taking on credit. There are also a lot of contradictions on this day – on one hand, we are likely to receive money, which is a good thing, but on the other, we will have to give some of it away, which is never particularly fun or pleasant. There is good reason to consider all of your opportunities and possibilities before acting.

It is not a good day to get married, as the wedding will not be as fun as you had hoped. However, the fourth lunar day is, in fact, a good day for sex and conceiving a healthy child.

Be careful on this day if you happen to engage in any physical exercise, as it is not a good idea to overeat or abuse alcohol. Take care of yourself. Any illnesses which began on this day may be extremely dangerous, if they are not dealt with immediately.

Cosmetic procedures are not contraindicated, as long as they are to preserve your appearance. Plastic surgery can be performed if you truly feel it is necessary.

However, avoid getting a haircut, as it is unlikely to grow back healthily, and will become brittle and dull. However, if the moon is in Leo, you can disregard this advice.

Dreams may turn out to be real.

The 5th lunar day.

Traditionally, the fifth lunar day is one of the worst of the lunar month. It is symbolized by a unicorn. Unicorns need to be tamed, but only a virgin is capable of doing so. Many people will feel drained on this day, or frustrated with themselves, those around them, and life in general.

Try to avoid arguments- any conflicts are likely to drag out for a long time, and then you may be overcome with guilt. This advice is relevant for both work and love.

Sexual encounters may be pleasant, but this is not a good day to plan a wedding, as it is likely to lead to a marriage full of unpleasant incidents.

Do not start any new businesses, or ask those around you for favors- you may be misunderstood and rejected.

It is fine to engage in physical exercise, but if you overdo it on this day, you may injure yourself.

Your energy levels are low. Cosmetic procedures may not be effective, and avoid any plastic surgeries.

It is good if you dream something connected with the road, trips or with movement in general. A bad dream might be a sign of a health problem which should be addressed.

The 6th lunar day.

The symbol of the sixth lunar day is a cloud and a crane. This is a philosophical combination that suggests that it is not worth rushing things on these days. This is a very positive, lucky day for both work and love. Creative work will be especially successful, as will any attempts at opening a new business in your field.

The sixth lunar day is a good time for resolving any financial matters. There is one limitation, however – do not give anyone a loan, as they may not pay it back. But you can certainly sponsor and support those who are more vulnerable than you.

This day is a good time to go on a trip, whether close to home or far away.

This is also a good day for dates, weddings, and marriage proposals. Remember that energy is more romantic than sexual, so it is better to give the gift of roses and a bottle of champagne than hot, passionate sex.

It is a good idea to get some exercise, but do not overdo things, though you will probably not want to, either.

Cosmetic procedures will be successful, and you can even have plastic surgery performed, so long as the moon is not in Scorpio.

It is still a good idea to avoid getting your hair cut, as you might "cut off" something good in addition to your hair.

It is better to not discuss dreams as they are usually true. Your dreams of this day can remind you of something that needs to be completed as soon as possible.

The 7th lunar day.

This is also a favorable lunar day, and it is symbolized by a fighting cock, which is an Avestan deity. Avoid any aggression on this day, and instead work on yourself, spend time at home or in nature. Avoid discussing the status of your relationship with anyone, arguing, or wishing bad things on anyone. Everything will come back to haunt you, remember, silence is golden.

Business negotiations and contracts will be successful. You can find support, sponsors, and people ready to help you in both words and deeds.

Lighten up with your colleagues and subordinates. Pay attention not only to their shortcomings, but also to their skills. This is a good day for reconciliation and creating both political and romantic unions.

The seventh lunar day is good for traveling, no matter how near or far from home.

It is also a favorable time for love and marriage.

Exercise moderately, and any plastic surgeries will go very smoothly, as long as the moon is not in Scorpio.

Dreams of this day may become a reality.

The 8th lunar day.

The symbol for this day is a Phoenix, which symbolizes eternal rebirth and renewal, because this day is a great time for changes in all areas of your life. Your energy is likely to be high, and you want to do something new and unusual. This is a good time to look for a new job or begin studying something. Any out-of-the-box thinking is welcome, along with shaking things up a bit in order to improve your life.

However, avoid any financial transactions, as you may incur losses.

Avoid aggression. You can share your opinion by presenting well-founded arguments and facts, instead.

The phoenix rises from the ashes, so this is a good time to be careful with electrical appliances and fire in general. The risk of housefires is high.

Avoid any major financial transactions on the eighth day, as you may end up facing a series of complications. You can pay people their salaries, as this is unlikely to be a large sum.

This is a good day for weddings, but only if you and your future spouse are restless, creative souls and hope to achieve personal development through your marriage.

Any cosmetic procedures and plastic surgeries will go well today, as they are related to rebirth and renewal. Surgeons may find that they are true artists on this day!

You can try to change your hairstyle and get a fashionable haircut on this day.

You can trust your dreams seen on this day.

The 9th lunar day.

The ninth lunar day is not particularly auspicious, and is even referred to as "Satan's" day. You may be overcome with doubt, suspicions, even depression and conflicts.

Your self-esteem will suffer, so don't overdo things physically, and avoid overeating or abusing alcohol.

This is a negative day for any business deals, travel, or financial transactions.

This is a particularly bad day for any events, so keep your head down at work and avoid any new initiatives.

It is better to avoid getting married on "Satan's" day, as the marriage will not last very long. Avoid sex, as well, but you can take care of your partner, listen them, and support them however they need.

Any cosmetic procedures will not have a lasting effect, and avoid any plastic surgery. A haircut will not turn out as you hoped.

Dreams of this day are usually prophetic.

The 10th lunar day.

This is one of the luckiest days of the lunar month. It is symbolized by a spring, mushroom, or phallus. This is a time for starting a new business, learning new things, and creating.

The 10th lunar day is particularly lucky for business. Networking and financial transactions will be a success and bring hope. This is an ideal time for changing jobs, shifting your business tactics, and other renewals.

This is a perfect time for people in creative fields and those working in science, who may come up with incredible ideas that will bring many successful returns.

This is a very successful day for building a family and proposing marriage. This is a good time for celebrations and communication, so plan parties, meet with friends, and plan a romantic date.

One of the symbols for this day is a phallus, so sexual encounters are likely to be particularly satisfying.

The 10th lunar day is the best time to begin repairs, buying furniture, and items for home improvement.

You can exercise vigorously, and cosmetic procedures and plastic surgery will be very effective.

Dreams of this day will not come true.

The 11th lunar day.

This is one of the best lunar days, and seen as the pinnacle of the lunar cycle. People are likely to be energetic, enthusiastic, and ready to move forward toward their goals.

The 11th lunar day is very successful for any financial transactions or business deals and meetings.

You might actively make yourself known, approach management to discuss a promotion, or look for a new job. This is an auspicious time for advertising campaigns, performances, and holding meetings.

Any trips planned will be a great success, whether near or far from home.

Romantic relationships are improving, sex is harmonious, and very desired.

Weddings held on this day will be fun, and the marriage will be a source of joy and happiness.

Exercise is a great idea, and you might even beat your own personal record.

This is an ideal time for any cosmetic procedures, but any more serious plastic surgeries might lead to a lot of bruising and swelling.

A haircut will turn out as you had hoped, and you can experiment a bit with your appearance.

You can ignore dreams of this day – usually they do not mean anything.

The 12th lunar day.

This day is symbolized by the Grail and a heart. As we move closer to the full moon, our emotions are at their most open. During this time, if you ask someone for something, your request will be heeded. This is a day of faith, goodness, and divine revelations.

For business and financial transactions, this is not the most promising day. However, if you help others on this day, your good deeds are sure to come back to you.

This is a day for reconciliation, so do not try to explain your relationships, as no one is at fault, and it is better to focus on yourself, anyway.

Avoid weddings and sex on this day, but if you want to do what your partner asks, there is no better time.

Many may feel less than confident and cheerful during this day, so take it easy when working out. Avoid overeating, stay hydrated, and avoid alcohol.

The 12th lunar day is not the best for getting married or having sex, but the stars would welcome affection and a kind word.

Avoid getting a haircut, or any plastic surgeries. This is a neutral day for minor cosmetic procedures.

Nearly all dreams will come true.

The 13th lunar day.

This day is symbolized by Samsara, the wheel of fate, which is very erratic and capable of moving in any direction. This is why the 13th lunar day is full of contradictions. In Indian traditions, this day is compared to a snake eating its own tail. This is a day for paying off old debts and returning to unfinished business.

Avoid beginning any new business on this day. It is preferable to finish old tasks and proofread your work. Information you receive on this day may not be reliable and must be verified.

It is worth resolving financial problems very carefully, and avoid arguments and conflict.

Do not change jobs on this day or go to a new place for the first time. Do not sit at home alone, though, go see old friends, parents, or older family members.

Minor cosmetic procedures are welcome on this day, but avoid any plastic surgery, as you may experience major swelling and bruising. Avoid any haircuts, too.

As a rule, all dreams will come true.

The 14th lunar day.

It's a full moon! The 14th lunar day is one of the happiest, and it is symbolized by the trumpet. Pay attention – you may run into new, much-needed information. Networking will be successful, and you can confidently sign agreements, meet with people, and attend fun gatherings or other leisure activities. This is one of the best days for advertising, performances, and concerts, and those working in creative professions should keep this in mind, as should those who work in politics. Do not sit in place on this day – you need to get out and see others, make new connections, and try to be visible.

This is one of the best days for communication with and making requests from management, as your initiatives will be noticed and welcome. You might talk about a promotion, raise, or something similarly related to professional growth.

Couples will see their relationship is moving along well on this day, and it is also a good day for getting married.

Any sex on this day will be vigorous and memorable for a long time. The full moon is the best time for conceiving a child.

Any cosmetic procedures will be effective, but avoid any major changes to your appearance, as there is a high likelihood of bleeding and bruising. A haircut will turn out well.

Your dreams of this day will be more or less doubtful.

The 15th lunar day.

It's a full moon! This day is symbolized by a serpent of fire. This is the energy peak of the entire lunar cycle, and a lot will depend on where you are focusing your energy.

You might face a lot of temptations on this day, for example, you might tell someone else's secret or your own to others, and come to regret it for a long time. The stars suggest exercising restraint in both your words and actions, as the 15th day of the lunar cycle is a day of deception and weaknesses.

This is a very active time, and many people might take unnecessary risks. This is not the best day for signing any agreements or contracts. For any performances, concerts, or advertising, however, this is one of the best days of the month.

You can get married on the 15th day, but only if you know each other well and have carefully considered your partnership, without any hasty decisions. This is also a favorable day for a second marriage.

Your romantic relationship is looking wonderful – you are on cloud 9, writing poetry, and deeply convinced of how right your partner is for you – and they feel the same way. It is important that this does not suddenly lead to an abrupt disappointment.

Avoid getting any haircuts on the 15th day of the month, as you may end up with a headache.

Conservative cosmetic procedures and creams will be very effective, but avoid any injections or plastic surgery today. Bleeding, swelling, and bruising are all but guaranteed.

Dreams on the 15th day nearly always come true.

The 16th lunar day.

This day is symbolized by a dove. The full moon is over, and the moon is now in its waning phase. Usually, after the turbulent days of the full moon, people feel a bit under the weather. They are not cheerful, and want to avoid excess worry and give themselves a chance to breathe.

Don't ignore your body's wishes, take it easy with physical activities, and take some time for yourself. You might spend time in nature, in the forest, or at a country home.

The 16th day of the lunar month is a time for moderation in all areas – your behavior, eating, and even in your clothes. If you overate during the full moon period, now is the time to diet a bit or at least avoid fatty foods and meat.

This is not a promising day for resolving any financial matters. Keep your documents in order and get ready for any future meetings, instead. If you help a loved one, your good deed will come back 100 times over.

Avoid getting married today, as well as sex.

Cosmetic procedures are likely to be a success, especially if they are related to cleansing your skin, but it is best to avoid any plastic surgery or injections. Your body is not ready to accept them. A haircut will turn out as you hoped.

Any dreams are likely to come true, but that also depends on a correct interpretation.

The 17th lunar day.

This day is represented by a vine and bell. It is a happy day and both successful and fun-filled. It is also a good time for negotiations, concluding small business deals, shaking up staffing, and creativity. However, you should keep in mind that the 17th day is only favorable for minor business, and you should avoid starting any major events.

Avoid any major financial transactions on this day. Do not give anyone money as a loan or borrow anything yourself, either.

Any travel, whether for business or pleasure, is likely to be a success.

The 17th day is a great time to get married, and an ideal day for dates. Any sexual encounters will bring you happiness and joy.

Avoid getting your hair cut on this day, but cosmetic procedures and plastic surgery will be a success. Women will look better than usual.

Your dreams are likely to come true in three days.

The 18th lunar day.

This day is represented by a mirror. It is a difficult, and generally unpromising day, too. Just as the mirror reflects our imperfections back to us, we need to remember that moderation and modesty are key.

The 18th day is not a favorable time for any business meetings or financial transactions. You can, however work on jobs you already began. It is, however, a positive day for those who work in research or the creative fields.

Your motto of the day is to keep a cool head when it comes to your opportunities and the opportunities of those around you. This is relevant for both work and romantic relationships. It is not a good time to criticize others – any conflicts or arguments may lead to lasting consequences, which you do not need.

Avoid getting married on this day, as well as sexual encounters, which are likely to be disappointing. It is a good time to take a trip together, which will only be good for your relationship.

Avoid getting your hair cut, though this is a relatively neutral day for a haircut, which might turn out well, and though it will not exceed your expectations, it will also not leave you upset. Avoid any plastic surgeries.

Dreams on this day will come true.

The 19th lunar day.

This is a very difficult day and it is represented by a spider. The energy is complicated, if not outright dangerous. Don't panic or get depressed, though – this is a test of your strength, and if you are able to hold onto all you have achieved. This is relevant for both work and love. On the 19th day, you should avoid taking any trips.

The energy of the 19th lunar day is very unfavorable for beginning any major projects, and business in general. Work on what you started earlier, get your affairs in order, think over your ideas and emotions, and check to make sure that everything you have done hitherto is living up to your expectations. Do not carry out any financial transactions or take out any loans – do not loan anyone else money, either. Do not ask your managers for anything as they are unlikely to listen to what you have to say, and make judgments instead.

This is a day when you might face outright deception, so do not take any risks and ignore rumors. Do not work on anything related to real estate or legal matters.

This is a very hard time for people with an unbalanced psyche, as they may experience sudden exacerbations or even suicidal ideations.

This is a very unlucky day to get married. Sexual encounters might be disappointing and significantly worsen your relationship.

Avoid any haircuts or cosmetic procedures or surgeries.

Your dreams of this day will come true.

The 20th lunar day.

This is also a difficult day, though less so than the 19th. It is represented by an eagle. This is a good time to work on your own development and spiritual growth, by speaking to a psychologist or astrologer.

Avoid pride, anger, arrogance, and envy.

The 20th lunar day is a good time for people who are active and decisive. They will be able to easily overcome any obstacles, flying over them just like an eagle. If you have to overcome your own fears, you will be able to do so – don't limit yourself, and you will see that there is nothing to be afraid of. It is a good day for any financial transactions, signing contracts, and reaching agreements, as well as networking.

The 20th lunar day is a favorable time for those who work in the creative fields, as they will be able to dream up the idea that will open up a whole host of new possibilities. Avoid conflicts – they may ruin your relationship with a lot of people, and it will not be easy to come back from that.

This is a lucky day for getting married, but only if you have been with your partner for several years, now. Sexual encounters will not be particularly joyful, but they also will not cause you any problems.

Avoid getting your hair cut, but you can certainly get it styled. The 20th lunar day is a good day for those who are looking to lose weight. You will be able to do so quickly, and it will be easy for you to follow a diet.

Cosmetic procedures will be a success, as will any plastic surgeries.

Pay attention to dreams of this day as they are likely to come true.

The 21st lunar day.

This is one of the most successful days of the lunar month, and it is symbolized by a herd of horses – imagine energy, strength, speed, and bravery. Everything you think up will happen quickly, and you will be able to easily overcome obstacles. A mare is not only brave but also an honest animal, so you will only experience this luck if you remember that honesty is always the best policy.

This is also a favorable day for business. Reaching new agreements and signing contracts, or dealing with foreign partners – it is all likely to be a success. Any financial issues will be resolved successfully.

Those in the creative world will be able to show off their talent and be recognized for their work. Anyone involved in the performing arts can expect success, luck, and recognition. A galloping herd of horses moves quickly, so you might transition to a new job, move to a new apartment, or go on a business trip or travel with your better half.

The 21st lunar day is one of the best to get married or have a sexual encounter.

This is a great time for athletes, hunters, and anyone who likes adventurous activities.

But for criminals and thieves, this is not a lucky or happy day – they will quickly be brought to justice.

Any haircuts or cosmetic procedures are likely to be a huge success and bring both beauty and happiness. You will recover quickly after any surgeries, perhaps without any swelling or bruising at all.

Dreams tend to not be reliable.

The 22nd lunar day.

This day will be strange and contradictory. It is symbolized by the elephant Ganesha. According to Indian mythology, Ganesha is the patron saint of hidden knowledge. so this is a favorable day for anyone who is trying to learn more about the world and ready to find the truth, though this is often seen as a hopeless endeavor. This is a day for philosophers and wisemen and women. However, it is an inauspicious day for business, and unlikely to lead to resolving financial issues, signing contracts, agreements, or beginning new projects. You can expect trouble at work.

For creative people, and new employees, this is a successful day.

This is a good day for apologies and reconciliation.

Avoid getting married, though you can feel free to engage in sexual encounters.

For haircuts and cosmetic procedures, this is a fantastic day. Surgeries will also turn out, as long as the moon is not in Scorpio.

Dreams will come true.

The 23rd lunar day.

This is a challenging day represented by a crocodile, which is a very aggressive animal. This is a day of strong energy, but it is also adventurous and tough. Your main task is to focus your energy in the right direction. There may be accidents, arguments, conflicts, fights, and violence, which is why it is important to strive for balance and calm.

Keep a close eye on your surroundings – there may be traitors or people who do not wish you well, so be careful.

However, this is still a favorable day for business – many problems will be resolved successfully. You are able to sign contracts and receive credit successfully, as long as you remain active and decisive in what you do.

This is not a day for changing jobs or working on real estate transactions or legal proceedings. This is not a favorable day for traveling, no matter how near or far you plan on going.

This is not a promising day to get married – things may end in conflict, if not an all-out brawl.

Sexual relations are not off the table, as long as the couple trusts one another.

Haircuts or cosmetic procedures will not turn out as you had hoped, so avoid them.

Dreams during this lunar day usually mean something opposite of what awaits you, so you can disregard them.

The 24th lunar day.

This is a neutral, calm day that is symbolized by a bear. It is favorable for forgiveness and reconciliation.

This is also a good day for learning new things, reading, self-development, and taking time to relax in nature.

This is a great day for any type of financial activity, conferences, academic meetings, and faraway travel.

The 24th lunar day is a good time for love and getting married, as any marriage will be strong and lasting.

Cosmetic procedures and plastic surgery will be a success, and you can expect a speedy recovery.

Avoid getting a haircut on this day, however, as your hair will likely thin and grow back slowly.

Dreams of this lunar day are usually connected with your personal life.

The 25th lunar day.

This is still another quiet day, symbolized by a turtle.

Just like a turtle, this is not a day to rush, and it is best to sit down and take stock of your life. This is a good time for resolving any personal problems, as the moon's energy makes it possible for you to calm down and find the right path.

This is also not a bad day for business. It is believed that any business you begin on this day is sure to be a success. This is especially the case for trade and any monetary activities.

The 25th lunar day is not a good day to get married, especially if the couple is very young.

This is a neutral day for sexual encounters, as the moon is waning, energy is low, so the decision is yours.

Avoid any cosmetic procedures, except those for cleansing your skin. This is not a favorable day for haircuts or plastic surgery – unless the moon is in Libra or Leo.

You can have a prophetic dream on this day.

The 26th lunar day.

The 26th lunar day is full of contradictions and complicated. It is represented by a toad.

It is not time to start or take on something new, as nothing good will come of it. Avoid any major purchases, as you will later come to see that your money was wasted. The best thing you can do on this day is stay at home and watch a good movie or read a good book.

Avoid traveling on this day, as it may not turn out well.

The 26th lunar day is a negative day for any business negotiations and starting new businesses. Do not complete any business deals or financial transactions. Your colleagues may be arguing, and your managers may be dissatisfied. But if you have decided to leave your job, there is no better time to do so.

This is not a good day to get married, as both partners' expectations may fall flat, and they will soon be disappointed.

The waning moon carries a negative charge, so avoid any haircuts and surgeries, though you can get cosmetic procedures if they are relatively minor.

Your dreams will come true.

The 27th lunar day.

The 27th lunar day is one of the best days of the month, and it is represented by a ship. You can boldly start any new business, which is sure to be promising. This is a great day for students, teachers, and learning new things. Any information that comes to you on this day may be extremely valuable and useful to you.

The 27th day is good for communication and travel, whether near or far from home, and no matter whether it is for work or pleasure.

This is also a good day for any professional activities or financial transactions. If there are people around you who need help, you must support them, as your good deeds will come back 100-fold.

Romantic dates will go well, though any weddings should be quiet and subdued. This is a particularly good day for older couples or second marriages.

The waning moon means that hair will grow back very slowly, but in general, you can expect a haircut to turn out well. This is a great day for plastic surgery or cosmetic procedures, as the results will be pleasing, and you will have a speedy recovery, without any bruising or swelling, most of the time.

However, beware if the moon is in Scorpio on this day – that is not a good omen for any plastic surgery.

Do not pay any attention to dreams on this day.

The 28th lunar day.

This is another favorable day in the waning moon cycle, and it is represented by a lotus. This is a day of wisdom and spiritual awakening. If possible, spend part of the day in nature. It is important to take stock of the last month and decide what you need to do during its two remaining days.

This is a good time for any career development, changing jobs, conducting business, decision-making, and signing agreements, as well as going on a trip. You might conclude any business deal, hold negotiations, work with money and securities.

This is also a good day for any repairs or improvements around your home or apartment.

Any weddings today should be subdued and modest, and restricted to family members only. A loud, raucous wedding might not turn out very well.

Your hair will grow slowly, but any haircuts will turn out very elegant and stylish. Cosmetic procedures and surgeries are not contraindicated. You will recover quickly with little bruising and swelling.

Do not take any dreams too seriously.

The 29th lunar day.

This is one of the most difficult days of the lunar month, and it is considered a Satanic day, unlucky for everyone and everything. It is symbolized by an octopus.

This is a dark day, and many will feel melancholy, depression, and a desire to simply be left alone. This is a day full of conflict and injuries, so be careful everywhere and with everyone. If you can, avoid any travel, and be particularly careful when handling any sharp objects. Do not engage in any business negotiations, sign any contracts, or take part in any networking.

Astrologers believe that anything you start on this day will completely fall apart. For once and for all, get rid of things that are impeding you from living your life. This is a good time to avoid people who you do find unpleasant.

This is also a time for fasting and limitations for everyone. Do not hold any celebrations, weddings, or have sexual relations – these events may not turn out as you hoped, and instead bring you nothing but suffering and strife.

Avoid getting a haircut, as well, as it will not make you look more beautiful and your hair will come back lifeless and dull. Cosmetic procedures can go ahead, but avoid any surgeries.

Dreams are likely to be true.

The 30th lunar day.

There is not always a 30th lunar day, as some lunar months have only 29 days. This day is represented by a swan. The 30th lunar day is usually very short, and sometimes, it lasts less than an hour. This is a time for forgiveness and calm.

You might take stock of the last month, while also avoiding anything you do not need around you. Pay back loans, make donations, reconcile with those who recently offended you, and stop speaking to people who cause you suffering.

This is a good time for tying up loose ends, and many astrologers believe that it is also a good day to start new business.

However, avoid celebrations or weddings on this day. Spouses will either not live long, or they will quickly grow apart.

Do not get a haircut on this day, though cosmetic procedures are possible, as long as you avoid any surgeries.

Dreams promise happiness and should come true.

A guide to Zodiac compatibility

Often, when we meet a person, we get a feeling that they are good and we take an instant liking to them. Another person, however, gives us immediate feelings of distrust, fear and hostility. Is there an astrological reason why people say that 'the first impression is the most accurate'? How can we detect those who will bring us nothing but trouble and unhappiness?

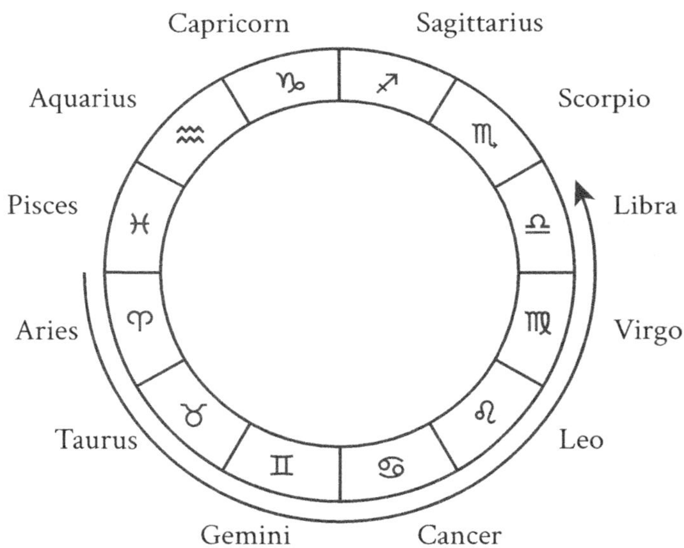

Without going too deeply into astrological subtleties unfamiliar to some readers, it is possible to determine the traits according to which friendship, love or business relationships will develop.

Let's begin with problematic relationships - our most difficult are with our **8th sign**. For example, for Aries the 8th sign is Scorpio, for Taurus it is Sagittarius and so on. Finding your 8th sign is easy; assume your own sign to be first (see above Figure) and then move eight signs counter clockwise around the Zodiac circle. This is also how the other signs (fourth, ninth and so on) that we mention are to be found.

Ancient astrologers variously referred to the 8th sign as the symbol of death, of destruction, of fated love or unfathomable attraction. In astrological terms, this pair is called 'master and slave' or 'boa constrictor and rabbit', with the role of 'master' or 'boa constrictor' being played by our 8th sign.

This relationship is especially difficult for politicians and business people.

We can take the example of a recent political confrontation in the USA. Hilary Clinton is a Scorpio while Donald Trump is a Gemini - her 8th sign. Even though many were certain that Clinton would be elected President, she lost.

To take another example, Hitler was a Taurus and his opponents – Stalin and Churchill - were both of his 8th sign, Sagittarius. The result of their confrontation is well known. Interestingly, the Russian Marshals who dealt crushing military blows to Hitler and so helped end the Third Reich - Konstantin Rokossovsky and Georgy Zhukov - were also Sagittarian, Hitler's 8th sign.

In another historical illustration, Lenin was also a Taurus. Stalin was of Lenin's 8th sign and was ultimately responsible for the downfall and possibly death of his one-time comrade-in-arms.

Business ties with those of our 8th sign are hazardous as they ultimately lead to stress and loss; both financial and moral. So, do not tangle with your 8th sign and never fight with it - your chances of winning are remote!

Such relationships are very interesting in terms of love and romance, however. We are magnetically attracted to our 8th sign and even though it may be very intense physically, it is very difficult for family life; 'Feeling bad when together, feeling worse when apart'.

As an example, let us take the famous lovers - George Sand who was Cancer and Alfred de Musset who was Sagittarius. Cancer is the 8th sign for Sagittarius, and the story of their crazy two-year love affair was the subject of much attention throughout France. Critics and writers were divided into 'Mussulist' and 'Sandist' camps; they debated fiercely about who was to blame for the sad ending to their love story - him or her. It's hard to imagine the energy needed to captivate the public for so long, but that energy was destructive for the couple. Passion raged in their hearts, but neither of them was able to comprehend their situation.

Georges Sand wrote to Musset, *"I don't love you anymore, and I will always adore you. I don't want you anymore, and I can't do without you. It seems that nothing but a heavenly lightning strike can heal me by destroying me. Good-bye! Stay or go, but don't say that I am not suffering. This is the only thing that can make me suffer even more, my love, my life, my blood! Go away, but kill me, leaving."* Musset replied only in brief, but its power surpassed Sand's tirade, *"When you embraced me, I felt something that is still bothering me, making it impossible for me to approach another woman."* These two people loved each other passionately and for two years lived together in a powder keg of passion, hatred and treachery.

When someone enters into a romantic liaison with their 8th sign, there will be no peace; indeed, these relationships are very attractive to those who enjoy the edgy, the borderline and, in the Dostoevsky style, the melodramatic. The first to lose interest in the relationship is, as a rule, the 8th sign.

If, by turn of fate, our child is born under our 8th sign, they will be very different from us and, in some ways, not live up to our expectations. It may be best to let them choose their own path.

In business and political relationships, the combination with our **12th sign** is also a complicated one.

We can take two political examples. Angela Merkel is a Cancer while Donald Trump is a Gemini - her 12th sign. This is why their relations are strained and complicated and we can even perhaps assume that the American president will achieve his political goals at her expense. Boris Yeltsin (Aquarius) was the 12th sign to Mikhail Gorbachev (Pisces) and it was Yeltsin who managed to dethrone the champion of Perestroika.

Even ancient astrologers noticed that our relationships with our 12th signs can never develop evenly; it is one of the most curious and problematic combinations. They are our hidden enemies and they seem to be digging a hole for us; they ingratiate themselves with us, discover our innermost secrets. As a result, we become bewildered and make mistakes when we deal with them. Among the Roman emperors murdered by members of their entourage, there was an interesting pattern - all the murderers were the 12th sign of the murdered.

We can also see this pernicious effect in Russian history: the German princess Alexandra (Gemini) married the last Russian Tsar Nicholas II (Taurus) - he was her 12th sign and brought her a tragic death. The wicked genius Grigory Rasputin (Cancer) made friends with Tsarina Alexandra, who was his 12th sign, and was murdered as a result of their odd friendship. The weakness of Nicholas II was exposed, and his authority reduced after the death of the economic and social reformer Pyotr Stolypin, who was his 12th sign. Thus, we see a chain of people whose downfall was brought about by their 12th sign.

So, it makes sense to be cautious of your 12th sign, especially if you have business ties. Usually, these people know much more about us than we want them to and they will often reveal our secrets for personal gain if it suits them. However, the outset of these relationships is, as a rule, quite normal - sometimes the two people will be friends, but sooner or later one will betray the other one or divulge a secret; inadvertently or not.

In terms of romantic relationships, our 12th sign is gentle, they take care of us and are tender towards us. They know our weaknesses well but accept them with understanding. It is they who guide us, although sometimes almost imperceptibly. Sexual attraction is usually strong.

For example, Meghan Markle is a Leo, the 12th sign for Prince Harry, who is a Virgo. Despite Queen Elizabeth II being lukewarm about the match, Harry's love was so strong that they did marry.

If a child is our 12th sign, it later becomes clear that they know all our secrets, even those that they are not supposed to know. It is very difficult to control them as they do everything in their own way.

Relations with our 7th **sign** are also interesting. They are like our opposite; they have something to learn from us while we, in turn, have something to learn from them. This combination, in business and personal relationships, can be very positive and stimulating provided that both partners are quite intelligent and have high moral standards but if not, constant misunderstandings and challenges follow. Marriage or co-operation with the 7th sign can only exist as the union of two fully-fledged individuals and in this case love, significant business achievements and social success are possible.

However, the combination can be not only interesting, but also quite complicated.

An example is Angelina Jolie, a Gemini, and Brad Pitt, a Sagittarius. This is a typical bond with a 7th sign - it's lively and interesting, but rather stressful. Although such a couple may quarrel and even part from time to time, never do they lose interest in each other.

This may be why this combination is more stable in middle-age when there is an understanding of the true nature of marriage and partnership. In global, political terms, this suggests a state of eternal tension - a cold war - for example between Yeltsin (Aquarius) and Bill Clinton (Leo).

Relations with our **9th sign** are very good; they are our teacher and advisor - one who reveals things we are unaware of and our relationships with them very often involve travel or re-location. The combination can lead to spiritual growth and can be beneficial in terms of business.

Although, for example, Trump and Putin are political opponents, they can come to an understanding and even feel a certain sympathy for each other because Putin is a Libra while Trump is a Gemini, his 9th sign.

This union is also quite harmonious for conjugal and romantic relationships.

We treat our **3rd sign** somewhat condescendingly. They are like our younger siblings; we teach them and expect them to listen attentively. Our younger brothers and sisters are more often than not born under this sign. In terms of personal and sexual relationships, the union is not very inspiring and can end quickly, although this is not always the case. In terms of business, it is fairly average as it often connects partners from different cities or countries.

We treat our **5th sign** as a child and we must take care of them accordingly. The combination is not very good for business, however, since our 5th sign triumphs over us in terms of connections and finances, and thereby gives us very little in return save for love or sympathy. However, they are very good for family and romantic relationships, especially if the 5th sign is female. If a child is born as a 5th sign to their parents, their relationship will be a mutually smooth, loving and understanding one that lasts a lifetime.

Our **10th sign** is a born leader. Depending on the spiritual level of those involved, both pleasant and tense relations are possible; the relationship is often mutually beneficial in the good times but mutually disruptive in the bad times. In family relations, our 10th sign always tries to lead and will do so according to their intelligence and upbringing.

Our **4th sign** protects our home and can act as a sponsor to strengthen our financial or moral positions. Their advice should be heeded in all cases as it can be very effective, albeit very unobtrusive. If a woman takes this role, the relationship can be long and romantic, since all the spouse's wishes are usually met one way or another. Sometimes, such couples achieve great social success; for instance, Hilary Clinton, a Scorpio is the 4th sign to Bill Clinton, a Leo. On the other hand, if the husband is the 4th sign for his wife, he tends to be henpecked. There is often a strong sexual attraction. Our 4th sign can improve our living conditions and care for us in a parental way. If a child is our 4th sign, they are close to us and support us affectionately.

Relations with our **11th sign** are often either friendly or patronizing; we treat them reverently, while they treat us with friendly condescension. Sometimes, these relationships develop in an 'older brother' or 'high-ranking friend' sense; indeed, older brothers and sisters are often our 11th sign. In terms of personal and sexual relationships, our 11th sign is always inclined to enslave us. This tendency is most clearly manifested in such alliances as Capricorn and Pisces or Leo and Libra. A child who is the 11th sign to their parents will achieve greater success than their parents, but this will only make the parents proud.

Our **2nd sign** should bring us financial or other benefits; we receive a lot from them in both our business and our family life. In married couples, the 2nd sign usually looks after the financial situation for the benefit of the family. Sexual attraction is strong.

Our **6th sign** is our 'slave'; we always benefit from working with them and it's very difficult for them to escape our influence. In the event of hostility, especially if they have provoked the conflict, they receive a powerful retaliatory strike. In personal relations, we can almost destroy them by making them dance to our tune. For example, if a husband doesn't allow his wife to work or there are other adverse family circumstances, she gradually becomes lost as an individual despite being surrounded by care. This is the best-case scenario; worse outcomes are possible. Our 6th sign has a strong sexual attraction to us because we are the fatal 8th sign for them; we cool down quickly, however, and often make all kinds of demands. If the relationship with our 6th sign is a long one, there is a danger that routine, boredom and stagnation will ultimately destroy the relationship. A child born under our 6th sign needs particularly careful handling as they can feel fear or embarrassment when communicating with us. Their health often needs increased attention and we should also remember that they are very different from us emotionally.

Finally, we turn to relations with **our own sign**. Scorpio with Scorpio and Cancer with Cancer get along well, but in most other cases, however, our own sign is of little interest to us as it has a similar energy. Sometimes, this relationship can develop as a rivalry, either in business or in love.

There is another interesting detail - we are often attracted to one particular sign. For example, a man's wife and mistress often have the same sign. If there is confrontation between the two, the stronger character displaces the weaker one. As an example, Prince Charles is a Scorpio, while both Princess Diana and Camilla Parker Bowles were born under the sign of Cancer. Camilla was the more assertive and became dominant.

Of course, in order to draw any definitive conclusions, we need an individually prepared horoscope, but the above always, one way or another, manifests itself.

Love description of Zodiac Signs

We know that human sexual behavior has been studied at length. Entire libraries have been written about it, with the aim of helping us understand ourselves and our partners. But is that even possible? It may not be; no matter how smart we are, when it comes to love and sex, there is always an infinite amount to learn. But we have to strive for perfection, and astrology, with its millennia of research, twelve astrological types, and twelve zodiac signs, may hold the key. Below, you will find a brief and accurate description of each zodiac sign's characteristics in love, for both men and women.

Men

ARIES

Aries men are not particularly deep or wise, but they make up for it in sincerity and loyalty. They are active, even aggressive lovers, but a hopeless romantic may be lurking just below the surface. Aries are often monogamous and chivalrous men, for whom there is only one woman (of course, in her absence, they can sleep around with no remorse). If the object of your affection is an Aries, be sure to give him a lot of sex, and remember that for an Aries, when it comes to sex, anything goes. Aries cannot stand women who are negative or disheveled. They need someone energetic, lively, and to feel exciting feelings of romance.

The best partner for an Aries is Cancer, Sagittarius, or Leo. Aquarius can also be a good match, but the relationship will be rather friendly in nature. Partnering with a Scorpio or Taurus will be difficult, but they can be stimulating lovers for an Aries. Virgos are good business contacts, but a poor match as lovers or spouses.

TAURUS

A typical Taurean man is warm, friendly, gentle, and passionate, even if he doesn't always show it. He is utterly captivated by the beauty of the female body, and can find inspiration in any woman. A Taurus has such excess physical and sexual prowess, that to him, sex is a way to relax and calm down. He is the most passionate and emotional lover of the Zodiac, but he expects his partner to take the initiative, and if she doesn't, he will easily find someone else. Taureans rarely divorce, and are true to the end – if not sexually, at least spiritually. They are secretive, keep their cards close, and may have secret lovers. If a Taurus does not feel a deep emotional connection with someone, he won't be shy to ask her friends for their number. He prefers a voluptuous figure over an athletic or skinny woman.

The best partners for a Taurus are Cancer, Virgo, Pisces, or Scorpio. Sagittarius can show a Taurus real delights in both body and spirit, but they are unlikely to make it down the aisle. They can have an interesting relationship with an Aquarius – these signs are very different, but sometimes can spend their lives together. They might initially feel attracted to an Aries, before rejecting her.

GEMINI

The typical Gemini man is easygoing and polite. He is calm, collected, and analytical. For a Gemini, passion is closely linked to intellect, to the point that they will try to find an explanation for their actions before carrying them out. But passion cannot be explained, which scares a Gemini, and they begin jumping from one extreme to the other. This is why you will find more bigamists among Geminis than any other sign of the Zodiac. Sometimes, Gemini men even have two families, or divorce and marry several times throughout the course of their lives. This may be because they simply can't let new and interesting experiences pass them by. A Gemini's wife or lover needs to be smart, quick, and always looking ahead. If she isn't, he will find a new object for his affection.

Aquarians, Libras, and Aries make good partners for a Gemini. A Sagittarius can be fascinating for him, but they will not marry before he reaches middle age, as both partners will be fickle while they are younger.

A Gemini and Scorpio are likely to be a difficult match, and the Gemini will try to wriggle out of the Scorpio's tight embrace. A Taurus will be an exciting sex partner, but their partnership won't be for long, and the Taurus is often at fault.

CANCER

Cancers tend to be deep, emotional individuals, who are both sensitive and highly sexual. Their charm is almost mystical, and they know how to use it. Cancers may be the most promiscuous sign of the Zodiac, and open to absolutely anything in bed. Younger Cancers look for women who are more mature, as they are skilled lovers. As they age, they look for someone young enough to be their own daughter, and delight in taking on the role of a teacher. Cancers are devoted to building a family and an inviting home, but once they achieve that goal, they are likely to have a wandering eye. They will not seek moral justification, as they sincerely believe it is simply something everyone does. Their charm works in such a way that women are deeply convinced they are the most important love in a Cancer's life, and that circumstances are the only thing preventing them from being together. Remember that a Cancer man is a master manipulator, and will not be yours unless he is sure you have throngs of admirers. He loves feminine curves, and is turned on by exquisite fragrances. Cancers don't end things with old lovers, and often go back for a visit after a breakup. Another type of Cancer is rarer – a faithful friend, and up for anything in order to provide for his wife and children. He is patriotic and a responsible worker.

Scorpios, Pisces, and other Cancers are a good match. A Taurus can make for a lasting relationship, as both signs place great value on family and are able to get along with one another. A Sagittarius will result in fights and blowouts from the very beginning, followed by conflicts and breakups. The Sagittarius will suffer the most. Marriage to an Aries isn't off the table, but it won't last very long.

LEO

A typical Leo is handsome, proud, and vain, with a need to be the center of attention at all times. They often pretend to be virtuous, until they are able to actually master it. They crave flattery, and prefer women who comply and cater to them. Leos demand unconditional obedience, and constant approval. When a Leo is in love, he is fairly sexual, and capable of being devoted and faithful. Cheap love affairs are not his thing, and Leos are highly aware of how expensive it is to divorce. They make excellent fathers. A Leo's partner needs to look polished and well-dressed, and he will not tolerate either frumpiness or nerds.

Aries, Sagittarius, and Gemini make for good matches. Leos are often very beguiling to Libras; this is the most infamous astrological "master-slave" pairing. Leos are also inexplicably drawn to Pisces – this is the only sign capable of taming them. A Leo and Virgo will face a host of problems sooner or later, and they might be material in nature. The Virgo will attempt to conquer him, and if she does, a breakup is inevitable.

VIRGO

Virgo is a highly intellectual sign, who likes to take a step back and spend his time studying the big picture. But love inherently does not lend itself to analysis, and this can leave Virgos feeling perplexed. While Virgo is taking his time, studying the object of his affection, someone else will swoop in and take her away, leaving him bitterly disappointed. Perhaps for that reason, Virgos tend to marry late, but once they are married, they remain true, and hardly ever initiate divorce. In bed, they are modest and reserved, as they see sex as some sort of quirk of nature, designed solely for procreation. Most Virgos have a gifted sense of taste, hearing, and smell. They cannot tolerate pungent odors and can be squeamish; they believe their partners should always take pains to be very clean. Virgos usually hate over-the-top expressions of love, and are immune to sex as a mean s of control. Many Virgos are stingy and more appropriate as husbands than lovers. Male Virgos tend to be monogamous, though if they are unhappy or disappointed with their partner, they may begin to look for comfort elsewhere and often give in to drunkenness.

Taurus, Capricorn, and Scorpio make the best partners for a Virgo. They may feel inexplicable attraction for Aquarians. They will form friendships with Aries, but rarely will this couple make it down the aisle. With Leos, be careful – this sign is best as a lover, not a spouse.

LIBRA

Libra is a very complex, wishy-washy sign. They are constantly seeking perfection, which often leaves them in discord with the reality around them. Libra men are elegant and refined, and expect no less from their partner. Many Libras treat their partners like a beautiful work of art, and have trouble holding onto the object of their affection. They view love itself as a very abstract concept, and can get tired of the physical aspect of their relationship. They are much more drawn to intrigue and the chase- dreams, candlelit evenings, and other symbols of romance. A high percentage of Libra men are gay, and they view sex with other men as the more elite option. Even when Libras are unhappy in their marriages, they never divorce willingly. Their wives might leave them, however, or they might be taken away by a more decisive partner.

Aquarius and Gemini make the best matches for Libras. Libra can also easily control an independent Sagittarius, and can easily fall under the influence of a powerful and determined Leo, before putting all his strength and effort into breaking free. Relationships with Scorpios are difficult; they may become lovers, but will rarely marry.

SCORPIO

Though it is common to perceive Scorpios as incredibly sexual, they are, in fact, very unassuming, and never brag about their exploits. They will, however, be faithful and devoted to the right woman. The Scorpio man is taciturn, and you can't expect any tender words from him, but he will defend those he loves to the very end. Despite his outward control, Scorpio is very emotional; he needs and craves love, and is willing to fight for it. Scorpios are incredible lovers, and rather than leaving them tired, sex leaves them feeling energized. They are always sexy, even if they aren't particularly handsome. They are unconcerned with the ceremony of wooing you, and more focused on the act of love itself.

Expressive Cancers and gentle, amenable Pisces make the best partners. A Scorpio might also fall under the spell of a Virgo, who is adept at taking the lead. Sparks might fly between two Scorpios, or with a Taurus, who is perfect for a Scorpio in bed. Relationships with Libras, Sagittarians, and Aries are difficult.

SAGITTARIUS

Sagittarian men are lucky, curious, and gregarious. Younger Sagittarians are romantic, passionate, and burning with desire to experience every type of love. Sagittarius is a very idealistic sign, and in that search for perfection, they tend to flit from one partner to another, eventually forgetting what they were even looking for in the first place. A negative Sagittarius might have two or three relationships going on at once, assigning each partner a different day of the week. On the other hand, a positive Sagittarius will channel his powerful sexual energy into creativity, and take his career to new heights. Generally speaking, after multiple relationships and divorces, the Sagittarian man will conclude that his ideal marriage is one where his partner is willing to look the other way.

Aries and Leo make the best matches for a Sagittarius. He might fall under the spell of a Cancer, but would not be happy being married to her. Gemini can be very intriguing, but will only make for a happy marriage after middle age, when both partners are older and wiser. Younger Sagittarians often marry Aquarian women, but things quickly fall apart. Scorpios can make for an interesting relationship, but if the Sagittarius fails to comply, divorce is inevitable.

CAPRICORN

Practical, reserved Capricorn is one of the least sexual signs of the Zodiac. He views sex as an idle way to pass the time, and something he can live without, until he wants to start a family. He tends to marry late, and almost never divorces. Young Capricorns are prone to suppressing their sexual desires, and only discover them later in life, when they have already achieved everything a real man needs – a career and money. We'll be frank – Capricorn is not the best lover, but he can compensate by being caring, attentive, and showering you with valuable gifts. Ever cautious, Capricorn loves to schedule his sexual relationships, and this is something partners will just have to accept. Women should understand that Capricorn needs some help relaxing – perhaps with alcohol. They prefer inconspicuous, unassuming women, and run away from a fashion plate.

The best partners for a Capricorn are Virgo, Taurus, or Scorpio. Cancers might catch his attention, and if they marry, it is likely to be for life. Capricorn is able to easily dominate Pisces, and Pisces-Capricorn is a well-known "slave and master" combination. Relationships with Leos tend to be erratic, and they are unlikely to wed. Aries might make for a cozy family at first, but things will cool off quickly, and often, the marriage only lasts as long as Capricorn is unwilling to make a change in his life.

AQUARIUS

Aquarian men are mercurial, and often come off as peculiar, unusual, or aloof, and detached. Aquarians are turned on by anything novel or strange, and they are constantly looking for new and interesting people. They are stimulated by having a variety of sexual partners, but they consider this to simply be normal life, rather than sexually immoral. Aquarians are unique – they are more abstract than realistic, and can be cold and incomprehensible, even in close relationships. Once an Aquarius gets married, he will try to remain within the realm of decency, but often fails. An Aquarian's partners need uncommon patience, as nothing they do can restrain him. Occasionally, one might encounter another kind of Aquarius – a responsible, hard worker, and exemplary family man.

The best matches for an Aquarius are female fellow Aquarians, Libras, and Sagittarians. When Aquarius seeks out yet another affair, he is not choosy, and will be happy with anyone.

PISCES

Pisces is the most eccentric sign of the Zodiac. This is reflected in his romantic tendencies and sex life. Pisces men become very dependent on those with whom they have a close relationship. Paradoxically, they are simultaneously crafty and childlike when it comes to playing games, and they are easily deceived. As a double bodied sign, Pisces rarely marry just once, as they are very sexual, easily fall in love, and are constantly seeking their ideal. Pisces are very warm people, who love to take care of others and are inclined toward "slave-master" relationships, in which they are the submissive partner. But after catering to so many lovers, Pisces will remain elusive. They are impossible to figure out ahead of time – today, they might be declaring their love for you, but tomorrow, they may disappear – possibly forever! To a Pisces, love is a fantasy, illusion, and dream, and they might spend their whole lives in pursuit of it. Pisces who are unhappy in love are vulnerable to alcoholism or drug addiction.

Cancer and Scorpio make the best partners for a Pisces. He is also easily dominated by Capricorn and Libra, but in turn will conquer even a queen-like Leo. Often, they are fascinated by Geminis – if they marry, it will last a long time, but likely not forever. Relationships with Aries and Sagittarians are erratic, though initially, things can seem almost perfect.

Women

ARIES

Aries women are leaders. They are decisive, bold, and very protective. An Aries can take initiative and is not afraid to make the first move. Her ideal man is strong, and someone she can admire. But remember, at the slightest whiff of weakness, she will knock him off his pedestal. She does not like dull, whiny men, and thinks that there is always a way out of any situation. If she loves someone, she will be faithful. Aries women are too honest to try leading a double life. They are possessive, jealous, and not only will they not forgive those who are unfaithful, their revenge may be brutal; they know no limits. If you can handle an Aries, don't try to put her in a cage; it is best to give her a long leash. Periodically give her some space – then she will seek you out herself. She is sexual, and believe that anything goes in bed.

Her best partners are a Sagittarius or Leo. A Libra can make a good match after middle age, once both partners have grown wiser and settled down a bit. Gemini and Aquarius are only good partners during the initial phase, when everything is still new, but soon enough, they will lose interest in each other. Scorpios are good matches in bed, but only suitable as lovers.

TAURUS

Taurean women possess qualities that men often dream about, but rarely find in the flesh – they are soft, charming, practical, and reliable – they are very caring and will support their partner in every way. A Taurus is highly sexual, affectionate, and can show a man how to take pleasure to new heights. She is also strong and intense. If she is in love, she will be faithful. But when love fades away, she might find someone else on the side, though she will still fight to save her marriage, particularly if her husband earns good money. A Taurus will not tolerate a man who is disheveled or disorganized, and anyone dating her needs to always be on his toes. She will expect gifts, and likes being taken to expensive restaurants, concerts, and other events. If you argue, try to make the first peace offering, because a Taurus finds it very hard to do so – she might withdraw and ruminate for a long time. Never air your dirty laundry; solve all your problems one-on-one.

Scorpio, Virgo, Capricorn, and Cancer make the best matches. A relationship with an Aries or Sagittarius would be difficult. There is little attraction between a Taurus and a Leo, and initially Libras can make for a good partner in bed, but things will quickly cool off and fall apart. A Taurus and Aquarius make an interesting match – despite the difference in signs, their relationships are often lasting, and almost lifelong.

GEMINI

Gemini women are social butterflies, outgoing, and they easily make friends, and then break off the friendship, if people do not hold their interest. A Gemini falls in love hard, is very creative, and often fantasizes about the object of her affection. She is uninterested in sex without any attachment, loves to flirt, and, for the most part, is not particularly affectionate. She dreams of a partner who is her friend, lover, and a romantic, all at once. A Gemini has no use for a man who brings nothing to the table intellectually. That is a tall order, so Geminis often divorce and marry several times. Others simply marry later in life. Once you have begun a life together, do not try to keep her inside – she needs to travel, explore, socialize, attend events and go to the theater. She cannot tolerate possessive men, so avoid giving her the third degree, and remember that despite her flirtatious and social nature, she is, in fact, faithful – as long as you keep her interested and she is in love. Astrologists believe that Geminis do not know what they need until age 29 or 30, so it is best to hold off on marriage until then.

Leo and Libra make the best matches. A relationship with a Cancer is likely, though complex, and depends solely on the Cancer's affection. A Gemini and Sagittarius can have an interesting, dynamic relationship, but these are two restless signs, which might only manage to get together after ages 40-45, once they have had enough thrills out of life and learned to be patient. Relationships with a Capricorn are very difficult, and almost never happen. The honeymoon stage can be wonderful with a Scorpio, but each partner will eventually go their own way, before ending things. A Gemini and Pisces union can also be very interesting – they are drawn to each other, and can have a wonderful relationship, but after a while, the cracks start to show and things will fall apart. An Aquarius is also not a bad match, but they may have little sexual chemistry.

CANCER

Cancers can be divided into two opposing groups. The first includes a sweet and gentle creature who is willing to dedicate her life to her husband and children. She is endlessly devoted to her husband, especially if he makes a decent living and remains faithful. She views all men as potential husbands, which means it is dangerous to strike up a relationship with her if your intentions are not serious; she can be anxious and clingy, sensitive and prone to crying. It is better to break things to her gently, rather than directly spitting out the cold, hard truth. She wants a man who can be a provider, though she often earns well herself. She puts money away for a rainy day, and knows how to be thrifty, for the sake of others around her, rather than only for herself. She is an excellent cook and capable of building an inviting home for her loved ones. She is enthusiastic in bed, a wonderful wife, and a caring mother.

The second type of Cancer is neurotic, and capable of creating a living hell for those around her. She believes that the world is her enemy, and manages to constantly find new intrigue and machinations.

Another Cancer, Virgo, Taurus, Scorpio, and Pisces make the best matches. A Cancer can often fall in love with a Gemini, but eventually, things will grow complicated, as she will be exhausted by a Gemini's constant mood swings and cheating. A Cancer and Sagittarius will initially have passionate sex, but things will quickly cool off. A relationship with a Capricorn is a real possibility, but only later in life, as while they are young, they are likely to fight and argue constantly. Cancer can also have a relationship with an Aries, but this will not be easy.

LEO

Leos are usually beautiful or charming, and outwardly sexual. And yet, appearances can be deceiving – they are not actually that interested in sex. Leo women want to be the center of attention and men running after them boosts their self-esteem, but they are more interested in their career, creating something new, and success than sex. They often have high-powered careers and are proud of their own achievements. Their partners need to be strong; if a Leo feels a man is weak, she can carry him herself for a while- before leaving him. It is difficult for her to find a partner for life, as chivalrous knights are a dying breed, and she is not willing to compromise. If you are interested in a Leo, take the initiative, admire her, and remember that even a queen is still a woman. Timid men or tightwads need not apply. Leos like to help others, but they don't need a walking disaster in their life. If they are married and in love, they are usually faithful, and petty gossip isn't their thing. Leo women make excellent mothers, and are ready to give their lives to their children. Their negative traits include vanity and a willingness to lie, in order to make themselves look better.

Sagittarius, Aries, and Libra make the best matches. Leos can also have an interesting relationship with a Virgo, though both partners will weaken each other. Life with a Taurus will lead to endless arguments – both signs are very stubborn, and unwilling to give in. Leos and Pisces are another difficult pair, as she will have to learn to be submissive if she wants to keep him around. A relationship with a Capricorn will work if there is a common denominator, but they will have little sexual chemistry. Life with a Scorpio will be turbulent to say the least, and they will usually break up later in life.

VIRGO

Virgo women are practical, clever, and often duplicitous. Marrying one isn't for everyone. She is a neat freak to the point of annoying those around her. She is also an excellent cook, and strives to ensure her children receive the very best by teaching them everything, and preparing them for a bright future. She is also thrifty – she won't throw money around, and, in fact, won't even give it to her husband. She has no time for rude, macho strongmen, and is suspicious of spendthrifts. She will not be offended if you take her to a cozy and modest café rather than an elegant restaurant. Virgos are masters of intrigue, and manage to outperform every other sign of the Zodiac in this regard. Virgos love to criticize everyone and everything; to listen to them, the entire world is simply a disaster and wrong, and only she is the exception to this rule. Virgos are not believed to be particularly sexual, but there are different variations when it comes to this. Rarely, one finds an open-minded Virgo willing to try anything, and who does it all on a grand scale – but she is rather the exception to this general rule.

The best matches for a Virgo are Cancer, Taurus, and Capricorn. She also can get along well with a Scorpio, but will find conflict with Sagittarius. A Pisces will strike her interest, but they will rarely make it down the aisle. She is often attracted to an Aquarius, but they would drive each other up the wall were they to actually marry. An Aries forces Virgo to see another side of life, but here, she will have to learn to conform and adapt.

LIBRA

Female Libras tend to be beautiful, glamorous, or very charming. They are practical, tactical, rational, though they are adept at hiding these qualities behind their romantic and elegant appearance. Libras are drawn to marriage, and are good at imagining the kind of partner they need. They seek out strong, well-off men and are often more interested in someone's social status and bank account than feelings. The object of their affection needs to be dashing, and have a good reputation in society. Libras love expensive things, jewelry, and finery. If they are feeling down, a beautiful gift will instantly cheer them up. They will not tolerate scandal or conflict, and will spend all their energy trying to keep the peace, or at least the appearance thereof. They do not like to air their dirty laundry, and will only divorce in extreme circumstances. They are always convinced they are right and react to any objections as though they have been insulted. Most Libras are not particularly sexual, except those with Venus or the Moon in Scorpio.

Leos, Geminis, and Aquarians make good matches. Libra women are highly attracted to Aries men – this is a real case of opposites attract. They can get along with a Sagittarius, though he will find that Libras are too proper and calm. Capricorn, Pisces, and Cancer are all difficult matches. Things will begin tumultuously with a Taurus, before each partner goes his or her own way.

SCORPIO

Scorpio women may appear outwardly restrained, but there is much more bubbling below the surface. They are ambitious with high self-esteem, but often wear a mask of unpretentiousness. They are the true power behind the scenes, the one who holds the family together, but never talk about it. Scorpios are strong-willed, resilient, and natural survivors. Often, Scorpios are brutally honest, and expect the same out of those around them. They do not like having to conform, and attempt to get others to adapt to them, as they honestly believe everyone will be better off that way. They are incredibly intuitive, and not easily deceived. They have an excellent memory, and can quickly figure out which of your buttons to push. They are passionate in bed, and their temperament will not diminish with age. When she is sexually frustrated, a Scorpio will throw all of her energy into her career or her loved ones. She is proud, categorical, and "if you don't do it right, don't do it at all" is her motto. Scorpio cannot be fooled, and she will not forgive any cheating. Will she cheat herself? Yes! But it will not break up her family, and she will attempt to keep it a secret. Scorpios are usually attractive to men, even if they are not particularly beautiful. They keep a low profile, though they always figure out their partner, and give them some invisible sign. There is also another, selfish type of Scorpio, who will use others for as long as they need them, before unceremoniously casting them aside.

Taurus is a good match; they will have excellent sexual chemistry and understand each other. Scorpio and Gemini are drawn to each other, but are unlikely to stay together long enough to actually get married. Cancer can be a good partner as well, but Cancers are possessive, while Scorpios do not like others meddling in their affairs, though they can later resolve their arguments in bed. Scorpio and Leo are often found together, but their relationship can also be very complicated. Leos are animated and chipper, while Scorpios, who are much deeper and more stubborn, see Leos as not particularly serious or reliable. One good example of this is Bill (a Leo) and Hillary (a Scorpio) Clinton. Virgo can also make a good partner, but when Scorpio seemingly lacks emotions, he will look for them elsewhere. Relationships with Lira are strange and very rare. Scorpio sees Libra as too insecure, and Libra does not appreciate Scorpio's rigidity. Two Scorpios together make an excellent marriage! Sagittarius and Scorpio are unlikely to get together, as she will think he is shallow and rude. If they do manage to get married, Scorpio's drive and persistence is the only thing that will make the marriage last. Capricorn is also not a bad match, and while Scorpio finds Aquarius attractive, they will rarely get married, as they are simply speaking different languages! Things are alright with a Pisces, as both signs are emotional, and Pisces can let Scorpio take the lead when necessary.

SAGITTARIUS

Sagittarius women are usually charming, bubbly, energetic, and have the gift of gab. They are kind, sincere, and love people. They are also straightforward, fair, and very ambitious, occasionally to the point of irritating those around them. But telling them something is easier than not telling them, and they often manage to win over their enemies. Sagittarius tends to have excellent intuition, and she loves to both learn and teach others. She is a natural leader, and loves taking charge at work and at home. Many Sagittarian women have itchy feet, and prefer all kinds of travel to sitting at home. They are not particularly good housewives – to be frank, cooking and cleaning is simply not for them. Their loved ones must learn to adapt to them, but Sagittarians themselves hate any pressure. They are not easy for men to handle, as Sagittarians want to be in charge. Sagittarius falls in love easily, is very sexual and temperamental, and may marry multiple times. Despite outward appearances, Sagittarius is a very lonely sign. Even after she is married with children, she may continue living as if she were alone; you might say she marches to the beat of her own drum. Younger Sagittarians can be reckless, but as they mature, they can be drawn to religion, philosophy, and the occult.

Aries and Leo make the best matches, as Sagittarius is able to bend to Leo's ways, or at least pretend to. Sagittarians often end up with Aquarians, but their marriages do not tend to be for the long haul. They are attracted to Geminis, but are unlikely to marry one until middle age, when both signs have settled down. Sagittarius and Cancer have incredible sexual chemistry, but an actual relationship between them would be tumultuous and difficult. Capricorn can make a good partner- as long as they are able to respect each other's quirks. Sagittarius rarely ends up with a Virgo, and while she may often meet Pisces, things are unlikely to go very far.

CAPRICORN

Capricorn women are conscientious, reliable, organized, and hard-working. Many believe that life means nothing but work, and live accordingly. They are practical, and not particularly drawn to parties or loud groups of people. But if someone useful will be there, they are sure to make an appearance. Capricorn women are stingy, but not as much as their male counterparts. They are critical of others, but think highly of themselves. Generally, they take a difficult path in life, but thanks to their dedication, perseverance, and willingness to push their own limits, they are able to forge their own path, and by 45 or 50, they can provide themselves with anything they could want. Capricorn women have the peculiarity of looking older than their peers when they are young, and younger than everyone else once they have matured. They are not particularly sexual, and tend to be faithful partners. They rarely divorce, and even will fight until the end, even for a failed marriage. Many Capricorns have a pessimistic outlook of life, and have a tendency to be depressed. They are rarely at the center of any social circle, but are excellent organizers. They have a very rigid view of life and love, and are not interested in a fling, as marriage is the end goal. As a wife, Capricorn is simultaneously difficult and reliable. She is difficult because of her strict nature and difficulty adapting. But she will also take on all the household duties, and her husband can relax, knowing his children are in good hands.

Taurus, Pisces, and Scorpio make good matches. Aries is difficult, once things cool off after the initial honeymoon. When a Capricorn meets another Capricorn, they will be each other's first and last love. Sagittarius isn't a bad match, but they don't always pass the test of time. Aquarius and Capricorn are a difficult match, and rarely found together. Things are too dull with a Virgo, and while Leo can be exciting at first, things will fall apart when he begins showing off. Libra and Aquarius are both difficult partners for Capricorn, and she is rarely found with either of them.

AQUARIUS

A female Aquarius is very different from her male counterparts. She is calm and keeps a cool head, but she is also affectionate and open. She values loyalty above all else, and is unlikely to recover from any infidelity, though she will only divorce if this becomes a chronic trend, and she has truly been stabbed in the back. She is not interested in her partner's money, but rather, his professional success. She is unobtrusive and trusting, and will refrain from listening in on her partner's phone conversations or hacking into his email. With rare exceptions, Aquarian women make terrible housewives. But they are excellent partners in life – they are faithful, never boring, and will not reject a man, even in the most difficult circumstances. Most Aquarians are highly intuitive, and can easily tell the truth from a lie. They themselves only lie in extreme situations, which call for a "white lie" in order to avoid hurting someone's feelings.

Aquarius gets along well with Aries, Gemini, and Libra. She can also have a good relationship with a Sagittarius. Taurus often makes a successful match, though they are emotionally very different; the same goes for Virgo. Aquarius and Scorpio, Capricorn, or Cancer is a difficult match. Pisces can make a good partner as well, as both signs complement each other. Any relationship with a Leo will be tumultuous, but lasting, as Leo is selfish, and Aquarius will therefore have to be very forgiving.

PISCES

Pisces women are very adaptable, musically inclined, and erotic. They possess an innate earthly wisdom, and a good business sense. Pisces often reinvent themselves; they can be emotional, soft, and obstinate, as well as sentimental, at times. Their behavioral changes can be explained by frequent ups and downs. Pisces is charming, caring, and her outward malleability is very attractive to men. She is capable of loving selflessly, as long as the man has something to love. Even if he doesn't, she will try and take care of him until the very end. Pisces' greatest fear is poverty. They are intuitive, vulnerable, and always try to avoid conflict. They love to embellish the truth, and sometimes alcohol helps with this. Rarely, one finds extremely unbalanced, neurotic and dishonest Pisces, who are capable of turning their loved ones' lives into a living Hell!

Taurus, Capricorn, Cancer, and Scorpio make the best matches. She will be greatly attracted to a Virgo, but a lasting relationship is only likely if both partners are highly spiritual. Any union with a Libra is likely to be difficult and full of conflict. Pisces finds Gemini attractive, and they may have a very lively relationship – for a while. Occasionally, Pisces ends up with a Sagittarius, but she will have to fade into the background and entirely submit to him. If she ends up with an Aquarius, expect strong emotional outbursts, and a marriage that revolves around the need to raise their children.

Tatiana Borsch

Printed in Great Britain
by Amazon

52195449R00056